HERE FOR A REASON

HERE FOR A REASON

Bill English: a Black Man's Journey
from Poverty to Corporate, Civic and
Social Justice Leadership

by Christina M. Cavitt and Geni Cavitt

Printed in the United States of America.

ISBN: 979-8-218-04648-4

Contents

INTRODUCTION

by Norb Berg, Retired Deputy Chair, Control Data Corporation

In 1969, Control Data Corporation (CDC) recruited Bill English to head our computer giant's revolutionary human resources affirmative action initiatives.

In all our dealings, I found Bill to be a dedicated change agent who demonstrated peaceful exchanges of values and views, consistently advocating the pursuit of a better world for all. He was modest, caring and demonstrated absolute integrity. He was courageous and blessed with an innate strategic mindset. He was never overly diplomatic, but possessed the right amount of diplomacy. He wasn't radical, but at the same time, was unafraid of what it took to make change happen.

Bill was tough about pursuing his causes. And make no mistake – he got things done. I never knew anybody in the community, Black or White, who stayed angry with him. They respected his values. They might not have agreed with him, but they could see the logic behind his actions.

To this day, Bill sets the standard for leadership in any community – residential, corporate, nonprofit – anywhere. After he joined the CDC team, I'd look around all the departments reporting to me and say, "When we have the caliber of people like Bill, let's set them up for success. Let's fill them with courage and knowledge and then provide

Bill and Norb

all the resources of a giant corporation to get their jobs done."

We needed Bill and others like him because they were integral to social change. None of our progress would have occurred at CDC and the world at large without people like Bill English patiently, tenaciously and even stubbornly pursuing it. Further, he managed to affect change without getting people angry.

He never gave up on his vision and while he wouldn't compromise, he gained credibility through strategic flexibility. Some of the minority employees that CDC executive management worked with were angry people. Bill, on the other hand, emanated, "Let's work through this together. Let's get it done."

I was impressed with Bill from the get-go. It's easy to come into any situation as a rabble rouser and aggravate everybody, to be effective at nothing except blocking progress. Bill wasn't that way. He made things happen because he advocated for collaboration through mutual respect. He had a vision which he presented openly and reasonably.

We share so many perspectives. I respect him because of his strong beliefs and incredible sense of fair play and balance. In turn, he respected others' beliefs.

Bill was a colleague who became a genuine friend. He's still affecting positive change in the Twin Cities.

Norb Berg

FORWARD

by Bill English

It is important to establish the fact that my life has been very complicated by and deeply engaged in issues regarding race and poverty. It is all of my experiences that have informed my thinking as an African-American man.

Initially, I was a reluctant participant in creating a book about me. I saw nothing exceptional about my life and my work. On the other hand, I know that being a productive citizen and member of the corporate world included being civically engaged and doing my job to the best of my ability. Not only that, I believe doing these things are God-given and constitutional responsibilities.

So why is what I've done deserving of a book? I was advised that my story might help others identify their personal role in making the world a better place. So I agreed to the publishing process.

My purpose in this book is to inspire young Black American men, and show them there are alternate paths for them. They simply have to make the right choices, like getting an education and working hard at a productive and satisfying career.

I won't spend a whole lot of time on my military days because I'm not a patriotic person in that regard. I want to focus much more on the positive things. But I'll be discussing the truth, because this book has to be genuine. While I plan to be authentic, it does not mean I have to share every detail of my life. Some things are private. As my grandmother instilled in me, "There are some things you don't share outside this house."

Leaving Illinois to enroll in college in Ypsilanti, Michigan, and later relocate to Minnesota, to finish my graduate degree and become the first Black salesman ever hired by 3M were major steps in my adult years. Next came the great opportunity to work for Control

Data, which ended up being the best career decision of my life.

To put things in context, I'll also include a few things about my upbringing and personal life. All of my experiences contributed to my becoming a servant leader in my home, profession and community.

So I invite you to sit back, pour your favorite beverage and join me as I reminisce. It's quite a journey for this American descendent of slavery.

PART 1

The Early Years

"Poverty and bigotry were a real part of my upbringing," Bill said. "But ethics, church, education and family support were integral to my childhood and the man I would one day become."

Bill (left) with brother Daniel Jr., circa 1942. When his youngest daughter first saw this photograph, she asked, "Daddy, was that slavery time?" "Why, no, Honey," Bill chuckled and gently explained, "That's just the way children dressed back in the 1940s."

CHAPTER 1

'No Negroes After 6 p.m.'

The 1940s seemed to be a simpler time. Not easier, but simpler. The decade was comfortable and safe, as long as everyone played by the rules. And there were strict rules governing William "Bill" English's childhood in Brooklyn, a.k.a. Lovejoy, Illinois, the oldest all-Black town in America.

Bill's hometown was founded in 1820, and incorporated in 1873, by enslaved people who swam across the Mississippi River from Missouri, which was a slave state, to the free state of Illinois. Those brave souls established the town, naming it for Elijah P. Lovejoy, an abolitionist newspaper publisher from nearby Alton, Illinois. As outrageous as it sounds today, back in the mid-1800s, slave traders snuck across the river to recapture free Negroes and punish Elijah. In 1837, a gang of vile criminals lynched Elijah and burned his newspaper to the ground. Many Black men died trying to protect him, but those who survived were successful in chasing the murderers back across the river.

Back in the days of slavery, Lovejoy residents were well-armed and slave-traders learned the hard way that the people of that town weren't about to return to a life of servitude. Furthermore, the U.S. government sent in troops to protect the town. Many decades later, in the late 1930s, only one White man lived in Brooklyn. His ancestor had worked for Elijah Lovejoy and came to town for his own safety after his employer was killed.

Bill's story begins

Bill was the firstborn of Dan and Lorene (nicknamed Lobie) English's children, joining the couple in the throes of the Great Depression on May 18, 1934. But for years, he thought he was born in 1936, because he was delivered by a midwife who delayed making her report until she could find the means to travel to the county seat. The family moved from Mariana, Arkansas, to Brooklyn when Bill was three years old.

Butting up against one side of town was Granite City. At the other end was East St. Louis and Belleville. Both Granite City and Belleville were all White communities and posted signs at their borders declaring, "No Negroes allowed after 6 p.m."

Seriously.

But within the town limits, young Bill felt completely safe.

"Everybody around me was Black," Bill recalled. "I was proud of that. Our business owners were Black, along with ministers and really, everybody in authority. The superintendent of schools was Black, as were all my classmates and teachers.

Bill's parents,
Dan and Lorene English

"Both Granite City and Belleville had steel mills where men from Brooklyn were employed," Bill explained. "If you worked the second shift, you were given passes, so when – not if, but when – the police stopped you, you could show them proof that you were a steel mill worker and they'd allow you to go about your business. Also, late-working domestics needed a permission slip from what we used to call 'Miss Ann.' That was the generic name for any White lady. 'Mr. Charlie' was our term for a White male who proffered a slip. If Black men or women didn't have a pass, they found themselves in a world of hurt."

Shotgun house

Like many U.S. families at that time, the Englishes were poor. But the kids never knew it. As far as they were concerned, they were just like all their neighbors. Bill joked that, "The saying was, 'We were so poor we couldn't buy a crippled flea a crutch.' But we didn't realize we were poor because everybody was the same. I was never hungry. We had a roof over our heads. We had parents who loved us. And we had fun! With all us children, there was never a dull moment."

The English home was a "shotgun house" – a narrow structure with rooms situated one behind the other and entrance doors at either end. They had running water, but Bill was a young teenager before the family upgraded to an indoor bathroom.

Two tragedies marked Bill's childhood. The first occurred when he was nine years old. The English house was heated by coal. One day, his mother stepped out to a neighbor's house for an errand and in the few minutes she was gone, the coal heater's pipe overheated and caught fire. The fire spread quickly and soon, the whole wooden structure was engulfed in flames.

"I had three younger siblings who weren't yet school age, and the oldest of them ordered everybody out, not realizing the baby was in the crib," Bill said. "And so we lost our six-month-old brother."

The second tragedy happened three years later, when a close friend drowned in the creek behind their row of houses.

"Those are the kinds of things that informed my life," Bill said. "Yet there was plenty of good, too. People were proud of our community. Everybody worked hard. Nobody had too much, but folks had enough to get by."

Example of a shotgun house

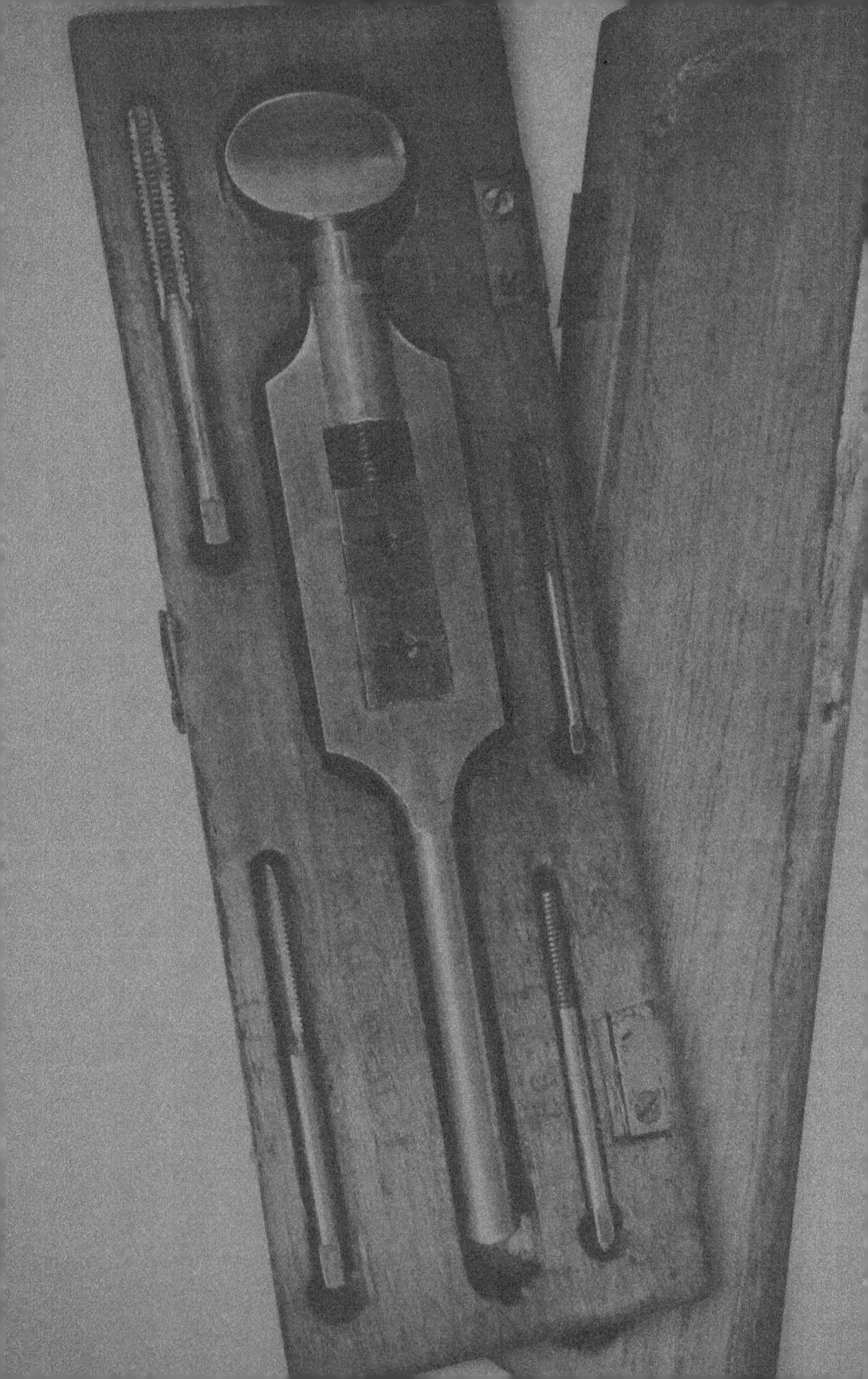

CHAPTER 2
Back Story

"My father dropped out of school after the eighth grade," Bill said. "He had to quit because Black kids attended school around cotton production. The crop had to be planted, then weeded at least twice, then picked. That's just the way it was – the way my parents were raised. They didn't complain about it. It wasn't fair, but it was far better than slavery, which their forebears endured. Dad could read and write well. At first, he taught himself, and then, with my mother's help, he became an extremely good reader."

Both of his father's parents were literate, too. The 1910 census has check marks in the columns indicating Bill's grandparents were "negro" and "could read and write." Further information about his predecessors is somewhat sketchy, because many records were destroyed in an Indianapolis fire around 1900. However, Bill was able to unearth some information from 1890 documents indicating his paternal grandfather and great-grandfather were both baptized "Daniel." His father had a twin, but the brother died at birth and was not named.

"My great-great-grandfather came from South Carolina, and was sold to someone in Arkansas," Bill recounted. "He married a woman (Liddy) who was sold from Georgia. We don't have a lot of details, but I always knew who they were. Family was paramount. We also knew about Great-Great-Grandfather's sister, Rebecca, who lived in their household, but any information about her fate as an adult is long lost. That happened a lot in Black families back then. People moved, some were sold…tragically, records were not always kept and oral histories were not always reliable."

The importance of grandparents

Bill's paternal grandfather died young of a heart attack. His paternal grandmother succumbed to tuberculosis. So Bill's dad was raised by his own grandparents. Bill's maternal grandparents also left his mother an orphan when she was seven years old, so she, too, was raised by her grandparents.

"My grandmother moved back in with her parents (Mary and Barry J. Ward) when my mom was seven," Bill explained. "My grandfather, Peter Lee, was a large man and light-skinned. Nicknamed 'Red,' he reportedly beat his wife, so eventually, she left him, taking my mother with her. By this time, Grandmother was very sick with TB and knew she was not long for this world. By moving in with her own parents before she died, my grandmother ensured the saftey of my mother.

"The last time Red saw my mother was several years later, when he was en route from Greenville, Mississippi, to Chicago, Illinois, and stopped in Marianna. He put $25 in his only child's hand and hugged her. Next, he apologized to Great-Grandmother for having mistreated my grandmother. He acknowledged that he had been wrong to hurt her and declared that he really did love his wife. Then he left and was never heard from again.

"He had no impact on my life," Bill continued. "He was just kind of a side story. On the other hand, I was blessed to know my great grandparents on my mother's side very well. My mother and her aunt Mahala, only five years older than she, were raised as sisters."

Bigwig leads family migration

"My oldest uncle, for whom I am named, was in the U.S. Army and fought in World War I," Bill said. "When he came home, he decided he wasn't going to live in Arkansas anymore. He packed up his family and moved to Illinois, where he'd landed a coveted steel mill job. He soon parlayed his high school diploma into a promotion as a timekeeper. That was an important role – he was kind of a bigwig. Further, he was the secretary of Brooklyn, which was an elected position."

After Dan and Lorene married, they followed Lorene's Uncle William to Illinois. At first, the steel mills weren't hiring, so Dan made his living as a furniture store porter. He hauled furniture, made customer deliveries and cleaned up the store. Eventually, possibly with the elder William's influence, but certainly through his own capabilities, Bill's father was offered a steel mill job.

William Ward, Bill's great uncle, along with wife Mattie, daughter Wilma and son Barry James.

"Dad began as 'chipper,' removing hot steel from around the molds before it hardened," Bill explained. "It was difficult and dirty labor, but he never shied away from hard work, especially to support his family. And he figured it was a good enough starting place. His dream was to become a tool and die maker. During his off time, he studied and trained with Black men who knew the trade. Unfortunately, back then, people of color weren't allowed to officially be tool and die makers. That simple. That was that. And so Dad lived and died wanting to be a tool and die maker."

Historic image of Brooklyn, EBONY magazine, 1952

CHAPTER 3
A World of Possibilities

"I was a good kid and enjoyed my classes," Bill said. "For me, school was a wonderful time.

"By and large, while I respected my dad, I was my mother's child. There's something uniquely special about the bond between a Black woman and her first-born son. I suppose she believed in me. For her, I represented the world of possibilities and opportunities that hadn't been available to her, but existed for a new generation. Every day, she'd tell me I was brilliant." In fact, Bill was very smart. He started reading when he was only four years old – well before he was enrolled in first grade.

"Mother 'altered the truth' about my age and put me in first grade a year before I was actually old enough," Bill noted. "My aunt worked for the school as an assistant teacher, qualified by her two years of study at Tuskegee Institute. Hers was a quasi-professional job. Because of her influence and the fact that my mother taught me to read early, she was able to get me in the classroom.

"I kept wondering why I was so much smaller than the rest of the kids in my grade," he laughed. "Later on, when I finally got a birth certificate, it seemed to became clear to me that I was born before the date on the document." His birth had been attended by a midwife. In the 1930s, Arkansas midwives had to register new babies at the county seat. The only way of traveling to the county seat was on the back of a mule, which she didn't own, so she had to wait many months to rent one for the journey. So not only my birth registration, but that of my little brother, who was a year and nine months my junior, were registered the same year. I didn't pay attention. I had no way to look at my birth certificate and they certainly didn't ask for formal documents when I was enrolled. The authorities just presumed parents were telling the truth."

Yet the truth wasn't far off. Lorene figured that because Bill was smart and could read, he'd be better off in school than stuck at home. No harm, no foul. Except for being a little shorter than his first-grade classmates, the young scholar flourished, earning straight A's through the eighth grade.

Little Bill walked into Lovejoy Elementary School amidst the din of hundreds of excited children, and the combined scent of floor wax, chalk on boards, Crayolas, pencil shavings and books. He was utterly engaged. He was captivated by the letters of the alphabet neatly printed and written in cursive above the blackboard. And he was mesmerized by his first grade teacher, Miss Amelia Cole.

"We kids honestly believed Miss Cole had eyes in the back of her head," Bill laughed. "We wished we could take her hair up and see them. What we didn't notice was that she had a mirror strategically placed so she could see what was going on amongst her charges while she wrote on the board. If we weren't paying attention, she always knew who was whispering or passing a note.

"Miss Cole insisted that you learn your alphabet," he said. "We had to learn how to do cursive writing in the first grade, too.

"Our books were always kind of raggedy," Bill continued in a more serious tone. "They were hand-me-downs from the White schools. Miss Cole taught us how to make book covers out of brown paper bags. And if you ever got a new book, oh, that was something to treasure!"

No matter the condition of the books, the children were taught to take good care of them. Otherwise, parents had to pay for replacements. As with children everywhere, the fear of an angry parent was an excellent motivator. Bill and his classmates were ever-diligent to carefully turn pages, avoid food spills and treat their books with great respect. None of this was a problem for Bill. He possessed a natural reverence for these "windows into the world." He loved reading and even as a young child, he saw the value of the stories and lessons words conveyed.

Lovejoy High School

CHAPTER 4
Educating Mind and Body

As Bill grew bigger and stronger, he developed into a good athlete. But sports always took a back seat to academic performance.

"My mother was a strict disciplinarian," Bill recalled. "A grade of B was not good enough for me. Anything less than an A was totally unacceptable. She allowed B for some of her kids, but nobody better make a C. If you came home with a C, you were in trouble. You'd be set on the porch before and after supper to study until your grades improved.

"I was strongly influenced by my mother." he said. "Every day, she assured me I was smart and good-looking, telling me, 'You're special and you're going to make something of yourself. You're going to do well.'" Bill didn't become arrogant with all this positive reinforcement. Rather, it built his self-esteem and sense of responsibility to do his best, no matter what.

Sing out

"You can't be Black and not like music," Bill explained. "It's so much a part of our natural culture. I grew up in the town that produced Miles Davis. Our school band director, George Hudson, was a great jazz trumpeter who came out of Kansas City. But he couldn't make a decent living at it, so he taught high school band and gigged on the side. In fact, Mr. Hudson hired Miles Davis, who was only 16 years old at the time, to play in his side job jazz band."

Bill didn't enroll in band. Instead, he expressed his musical talents by adding his clear and strong tenor voice to the high school's choir.

"I'm not a trained musician," Bill said. "It's just something that I took up in high school. My teacher told me I had a tenor voice, so that's the section I sang with. When I moved to the Twin Cities, I joined a church choir. Unfortunately, cigarette smoking got to my voice." Bill noted that smoking was the most addictive thing he ever experienced and overcame in his life.

"Even though I didn't play an instrument – or you might say that voice was my instrument – the entire school enjoyed our band director's professional musical connections when he brought in jazz greats like Billie Eckstein and Sarah Vaughan," Bill recalled. "Mr. Hudson knew these stars because he grew up playing music with them in Pittsburgh."

Although Bill was more interested in music and studies than sports, he could hold his own on the basketball court and the track at Lovejoy Junior and Senior High Schools. Bill graduated salutatorian in 1951.

"Ruby Dale was top of our class and beat me out, and happened to be my best friend," Bill said. "May she rest in peace. We walked to school together every day, and we were always challenging each other. We studied a lot with one another. The reason she beat me was because I got a B in industrial arts. I will never forget our industrial arts teacher, Mr. Ned Carson Brown. He came from Tuskegee University, where I later recruited employees for Control Data. Anyway, I'll never forget what he told me one day."

"English!" the teacher commanded, drawling out Bill's last name with a deep southern accent.

"Yes, Mr. Brown?" Bill responded.

"You got a reputation of being one of the smartest boys in this school — maybe the smartest," Mr. Brown said.

"Thank you, sir," Bill replied. "I'm proud of that and I work hard."

"Well, you're about to flunk my course," Mr. Brown declared. "Son, in order to pass Shop One, you've got to make a lamp. To do that, you've got to do a floor drawing and work a lathe. But you can't draw a straight line with a T-square. And work a lathe? Forget about it."

"I knew Mr. Brown was giving it to me straight, but I didn't like it," Bill reflected. "I needed the industrial arts credit, so I decided I was going to cheat. I wasn't a cheater, but I did that time. I cut deals. The classmate who drew my floor plan got my biology test answers – the fellow who built my lamp got my answers in algebra. I'd pretend I was hard at work on that lathe as long as Mr. Brown was looking. As soon as he'd leave the room, I'd jump off and another guy jumped on it. Mr. Brown was smart, but somehow, we pulled the wool over his eyes and I got by with the only B on my high school transcript."

At the end of the semester, Mr. Brown called out to Bill as he exited the shop classroom, "Boy, I don't know how you earned a B, but you did it. However, I don't trust this B. I think you cheated, but I can't prove it. I'll be watching you very carefully in Shop Two."

"Oh, yes, sir." Bill responded with a wry smile, knowing full well he wouldn't take Mr. Brown's next level class. Instead, he signed up for home economics, "Where the girls were. I was the only boy in home ec.," Bill fondly recalled. "The next year, so many boys tried getting in that elective that the administration turned them down. But I got by and did pretty well baking cookies that people could smell throughout the whole school. I never did learn how to sew, but the girls would thread my little machine and produce my required project – an apron. And I was happy around a bunch of women. I'm still that way."

English, American literature, economics, civics and geography filled Bill's days and he loved every minute of learning. His curiosity was finely tuned and his mind open to expansion. Even penmanship was graded.

"I'm sad when I see these kids now who can't write cursive. I had beautiful handwriting in my day, but a slight tremor in my right hand has diminished it.

"I wanted to know everything there was to learn," Bill added. "My mother told me, 'You pick up as much as you can about the world – the places you're in, how to solve math, and how to write and speak English correctly. All of these things matter, young man. You mark my words.'"

'NITNB'

"Indeed, all of those things have always mattered deeply to me and my family," Bill stated. "My brother, Daniel Jr., a year younger than I, fell through the cracks in his first year at school. But Mom so valued real learning that she made the difficult decision to make him take first grade over again. That was the right thing for him scholastically, but it was very hard on him socially. He never let my mother forget it. I don't think he ever really forgave her for her uncompromising tough love. But it really was for the better."

The kids were home for the summer and their mother was sitting on the front porch when Bill and Dan arrived with report cards. Bill's card noted he'd been promoted to the third grade. Dan's marks indicated that he was going on to second grade. Lorene had been suspicious about the effectiveness of Dan's education and decided to test her second son.

"Spell your name, Daniel," Lorene demanded.

"N-I-T-N-B," Dan recited.

"What did you say?" Lorene queried, rapping his hands, fetching her purse and admonishing him, *"Come on with me!"* With that, she marched him right back to Lovejoy Elementary to confront Fidella Gates, the woman charged with teaching Dan's first grade class.

"Fidella!" she exclaimed.

"Yes, Lorene, what is it?" Ms. Gates replied, with growing concern.

"You had my son here all year long," Lorene accused. *"Ask him to spell his name. Go ahead, just ask him."* Ms. Gates did, and Dan shyly repeated the letters, *"N-I-T-N-B."* The truth was evident. Dan hadn't learn to spell.

"Daniel has been such a good kid all year," Ms. Gates sheepishly defended herself. *"I didn't realize there was any problem."*

"Look, Fidella, all of my kids are good kids," Lorene said, calming down a bit. *"I'm not talking about his behavior. I'm talking about what he learned,"* she said, shifting her attention to the now very uncomfortable little

boy. "Son? Do you know what two and two is?"

"Four," Dan answered, without hesitation.

"Well, at least he learned to add a little bit," Lorene said. "But what else did you do with him all year? He can't spell his name. You're going to have him again next year. Don't let him come out the same way, because if you do, I will come looking for you."

Eventually, Ms. Gates admitted that because Dan was so nice and he was cute and he played up to her and charmed her a little bit, she'd let him get by. But Lorene English was not having any of it. So Dan repeated the first grade, coming out knowing how to spell.

Enemy gender

"I remember hearing about when Japanese forces attacked Pearl Harbor in 1941," Bill recalled. "Reporters referred to Japan as a 'she' who had attacked us. Well, at that young age, I'm thinking Japan was a woman. I was six years old. All I knew was that we were at war.

"My father's brother, Roger Vesky English, was in the Navy at the time and I heard my parents talk about him," Bill said. "He hadn't been stationed in Hawaii, but was involved in fighting the Germans. Again, Germany was assigned female gender. It was all pretty confusing to me. I didn't quite understand who we were fighting. Then again, I was not exactly interested. The war was far away from my little kid realities, like school, how I could earn a penny for a piece of candy or what games my friends and I would play at recess."

As WWII raged on and Bill grew into his early teens, he realized that women weren't the enemy. Rather, it was ignorance and hatred that fueled global conflict. So he did his bit for the war effort. He and his buddies collected scrap metal, saved foil from their chewing gum wrappers, collected string, obeyed the lights-out mandates – that sort of thing.

Of course, the children of his town weren't allowed to run wild. Within a six block radius, the English's neighbors were like a close-knit, extended family.

"Anybody in the neighborhood could whip your behind if you got caught doing something wrong, and that was a-okay with our parents," Bill noted. "And then they'd call Mom or Dad on the party line and we'd come home to a second strapping. It didn't seem entirely fair to us kids, but really, it was just a matter of folks looking out for one another."

Still, even the most diligent adult supervision couldn't possibly keep the young ones safe all the time.

"We used to go junkin' – picking up scrap iron, glass and things needed for the war effort. It was legitimate work for kids back then. We could earn a few dollars on the weekend and help support our soldiers. We also whitewashed trees in the White neighborhoods. It was okay for us to cross the East St. Louis city limits during the day. We just couldn't be there at night.

"We'd mix chalk and water to paint the trunks of the trees," Bill explained. "Everybody liked white trunks on their trees. The contrast of that with green leaves made it quite attractive. We'd charge a nickel for a small tree, medium trees were a dime, and fat trees cost 15-cents. But every time it rained, we'd have to go back and do it again. That was a money-maker for us in the spring and summer.

"The White kids knew what we were there for," Bill continued. "We went about our business. They didn't bother us and we didn't bother them. They weren't allowed to speak to us or play with us. We didn't care. We were there to make money."

NOTE: Bill grew up near the Missouri and Illinois border. Back then, police forces, fire departments, stores, schools – everything – was segregated. On the other hand, "The mafia influenced everybody equally," Bill said. "In fact, my best friend's father was an accountant for the mob. He was smart and could have been an asset to any legitimate business, but no white-owned business would hire a Black man back then. It wasn't always acknowledged in polite company, but the mafia had a lot of influence on both sides of the border."

Church choices

Bill's mother was raised African Methodist Episcopal (AME) and initially attended Lovejoy's oldest church, Quin Chapel (named for a forefather of the African American Episcopalian Church), until she joined her husband's Baptist church, Southern Tabernacle. She later converted to a more fundamentalist Pentecostal practice. The couple let their children chose which faith to follow, but the children had to attend services every single Sunday. The Baptist community resonated with Bill, so that's where he went.

"Church was an all-day affair," Bill recalled. "We'd start the day with a quick wash and put on our best clothes for Sunday school, which started at 9 a.m. sharp, right before the 11 a.m. service. Then we'd go home for dinner and back to church for the Baptist's Young People's Union (BYPU) meeting. That was very interesting for me, because we learned not only about scripture, but African-American history, too. Remember, the school books didn't contain any Black history. Slavery was glossed over, at best, in American history books.

"Also, we were taught poetry and played academic games, led by young teachers," Bill continued. "They wrote Easter and Christmas speeches for us to memorize for programs. Because I could remember two pages, I had to read the longest poems in the church. But I now understood that was their way of keeping me busy and engaged in some form of education."

Required studies

When it came to required studies, Bill was all business. And he allowed the best of his teachers to leave their indelible mark on his mind, and in some cases, his heart. His remarkable teachers included his first-grade teacher, Amelia Cole (the woman with eyes in the back of her head), and Mrs. Cecil Hudspeth Oliver, the principal.

Also, Bill's outstanding educators included:

- **Mr. Alfred Clark**, fifth grade
- **Ms. Lynelle Weaver**, sixth grade
- **Ms. Ewing**, seventh grade

Mr. Ezra Turner, poet, eighth grade economics, civics and literature, "Was one of the most gifted teachers I've ever encountered," Bill stated.

"He grew up in Missouri and attended Lincoln University. At the time, that was one of the only higher education options for people of color. He encouraged us to question commonly held beliefs concerning American history. For instance, authorities claimed that Columbus discovered America, but Mr. Turner asked, 'What about all the people who were already here? Maybe Columbus was the first European to accidentally bump his ships onto our shores, bringing gifts of cheap trinkets and smallpox. But he didn't discover anything. The land was already populated.'

"One time, Mr. Turner caught me kissing a girl in the cloakroom, and he admonished me about disrespecting her," Bill recalled. "He told me no gentleman would ever do that. And he insisted that I apologize. Now, she was as guilty as I was, but he put it all on me. I don't know why. But what he was really trying to teach me was to respect women. Ezra Turner had a huge impact that I didn't realize until much later in my life."

Bill's senior portrait

Mr. Turner introduced his students to Paul Lawrence Dunbar, whose internationally recognized writing in dialect deeply moved Bill and set him on a lifelong love of poetry. He also taught that "Africa wasn't Tarzan swinging in the jungle, that Timbuktu was a center of great learning and about the horrific cultural aspects and horrors of American slavery. Further, he filled us in on truths like the fact that a Negro invented the cotton gin, not Eli Whitney, and the famous explorers Lewis and Clark included a Black freedman among their discovery entourage."

Mr. Turner published a poetry book entitled *An Ode to Phillipa*, about Phillapa, daughter of George Skyler (a Booker Washington-esque columnist for *The Pittsburgh Courier*, the only black nationwide distributed newspaper).

Ms. Jason, high school world, American, Illinois and Negro history

"Ms. Jason had a unique way of engaging us in the past," Bill said. "In our town, both boys and girls played baseball, or at least understood the game. Depending upon the difficulty of questions she raised after each chapter and the quality of our answers, she'd give us a single, double, triple or home run rating. That appealed to our interest in ball and our competitive natures. And it worked."

Ms. Griffin, high school language arts

"She taught us that if we wanted to be taken seriously in a predominantly White world, we'd best learn how to use broadly-accepted grammar and punctuation, and to write well-thought-out paragraphs," Bill recalled. "To get a good grade from her, we had to study hard. Ms. Griffin's lessons stay with me to this day."

Also included in Bill's memorable influences was **Mr. Ernie Page**, "My high school basketball coach, who had a profound impact on the person I would become," Bill said. "He told me that while I wasn't the top athlete in the world, I was the best at learning plays and disciplined enough to execute them. That's why I got a chance to play often. I understood that basketball wasn't just about scoring points. Learning how to make others better is what it was all about."

The Old Front Gate
BY PAUL LAURENCE DUNBAR

W'en daih's chillun in de house,
Dey keep on a-gittin' tall;
But de folks don' seem to see
Dat dey's growin' up at all,
'Twell dey fin' out some fine day
Dat de gals has 'menced to grow,
W'en dey notice as dey pass
Dat de front gate's saggin' low.
W'en de hinges creak an' cry,
An' de bahs go slantin' down,
You kin reckon dat hit's time
Fu' to cas' yo' eye erroun',
'Cause daih ain't no 'sputin' dis,
Hit's de trues' sign to show
Dat daih's cou'tin goin' on
W'en de ol' front gate sags low.
Oh, you grumble an' complain,
An' you prop dat gate up right;
But you notice right nex' day
Dat hit's in de same ol' plight.
So you fin' dat hit's a rule,
An' daih ain' no use to blow,
W'en de gals is growin' up,
Dat de front gate will sag low

the poem that set Bill on a lifelong love of poetry

Rev. Dr. Henry O. Hardy, Retired Minister

Retired Rev. Dr. Henry O. Hardy and Bill hail from the same hometown of Lovejoy. The retired minister is a south side of Chicago author and retired "pastoral powerhouse," states a 2002 article by A. L. Smith, contributing writer to The Crusader Newspaper Group. Bill is a couple years older, so Henry said, "I've known him all my life."

Henry's family lived down the street from the English household and he spent a lot of time with the neighborhood kids making their way into Lorene's kitchen. He had been buddies with Bill's little brother, Thomas.

"I think I spent as much time at the English home as I did my own," Henry recalled, adding with a laugh that, "One didn't cross Mrs. Lorene English. You couldn't get away with anything with her. She was a stern disciplinarian, and not just with her own kids. But if you obeyed the rules and were polite, you got along just fine.

"By virtue of Bill's being older, a good athlete and a great student, he was naturally somebody we 'little kids' looked up to," Henry said. "Also, being right across the river from East St. Louis and big city clothing stores, Lovejoy was kind of a hip town. Back in the day, Bill and the older guys were fashionable. In fact, Bill remains an impeccable dresser."

Henry lost track of the English children after graduating from high school. Then, during his studies at the University of Chicago in the early 1960s, he came to Minneapolis for a 12-month ministry internship. He'd just arrived and happened to be at the downtown Minneapolis Public Library when he spied a familiar face across the bookshelves and worktables. It was none other than Bill English! The two of them became reacquainted and Bill invited the young divinity student to stay in his home. Over the years, the two men became close. Henry presided over Bill and Freddie's wedding, and Henry came to one of Bill's daughter's weddings. Bill, in turn, was Henry's best man at his wedding in Chicago. Also, Bill spoke at Henry's retirement.

"I spoke at his mother's transitional service in Lovejoy when she passed," Henry said. "I also spoke during two of his brother's funeral services in New York."

"I'm very proud of Bill," Henry stated. "As the first African American vice present at a Fortune 500 company, Control Data Corporation, he is an East St. Louis area success story. He is not one restricted by roots or environment, prejudicial assessments of individuals based on locale or upbringing. Bill came through and represents. Furthermore, Bill is a man of high intellect. A deep thinker. A community leader. A politically astute player. A progressive entrepreneur in bringing business to North Minneapolis. Bill has a voice and knows how to use it. He is always engaged and trying to have an enlightened impact on his community."

While Henry recognizes the serious side of Bill, he isn't afraid to point out that, "Bill isn't always as time conscious as others. One time, he was taking me to the airport after a visit in Minneapolis and I was starting to get a little nervous when the time was getting closer to my departure and we still hadn't left his house. Finally, we got in the car.

"'Don't worry,' Bill assured me. 'We have plenty of time.' Well, it was a heart-in-my-mouth freeway drive to get there. We zoomed down the onramp, immediately got stuck in a traffic jam and ended up arriving at the airport at the very last minute. Bill remained calm while I had heart palpitations! I jumped out of his car, grabbed my bag and literally sprinted through the airport. This was before 9-11 and all the security checks, etc. Anyway, I got to my gate just before they closed the jetway. I sat down and had to smile. Yep, that's my friend, Bill. Just in time!"

CHAPTER 5
Life at 700 Adams Street

"I was always listening to radio news," Bill said. "Through those broadcasts, I became very much aware that the world was vastly larger than my little hometown. My parents were dyed-in-the-wool Democrats. All they talked about was President Roosevelt and the good he did. Despite that, my daily reality was rooted in hometown life.

"We were a mix of urban and country. There was a big farm less than a mile away. There were nearby stockyards too. Armor and Swift packing houses were huge in East St. Louis back then. And we had the steel mills going full blast because of the war effort. My earliest memories include playing with my friends, who all had home chores to do. Everybody worked hard, even the children. For instance, most families kept chickens in their back yards that had to be fed, slaughtered, boiled and plucked. Eggs needed gathering, dishes washed, laundry cleaned, wood chopped, porches scrubbed and dirt in the yards raked. Grass lawns were too expensive to maintain, so each day, we arranged the soil to appear neat. As the oldest child in a large family, I learned to do everything, including looking after my siblings – changing diapers, feeding the babies and setting the example for the young ones."

Bill's favorite holiday was Christmas. Every year, the English's family room was transformed into a fantasy-land with a big tree, festooned with lights and ornaments.

"We always had a special dinner on Christmas Day," Bill recalled. "Mom outdid herself preparing a roasted turkey or ham, and she assembled the world's most delicious fruit salad. Every one of us kids has tried recreating her concoction, but I've never quite hit the mark. And she made a caramel cake that was so good 'It would make you smack your grandmother' [for making such bad cakes]. That was one of the expressions we used. I guess it was kind of a cultural saying, like, 'I'll see you next week, God willin' and the creek don't rise.'"

Lorene made sure her family enjoyed plentiful Christmases. She would start shopping at the 10-cent store early in the year and put items on layaway so that by Christmas morning, every child had at least two toys and much needed new clothes. There were too many brightly wrapped packages to fit under the tree, so the children were each assigned a section on the couch or chair where they'd find their presents. One year, Bill's parents gave him a brand new purple Monarch bicycle that he absolutely loved.

"I vividly remember that bike," he said. "Sadly, I only got to ride it a few times because when the house burned down, my bike was in it. We didn't have insurance on the house or its contents, of course. Insurance was a luxury nobody we knew could afford. But with the help of family and neighbors, my parents rebuilt. We rented a house across from my uncle's place down the street until construction was completed."

Farewell, George

One day when the trees were all whitewashed, Bill and his buddies had agreed that they'd meet up, ostensibly to go junking, but they were really going to go swimming.

"Georgie McCoy, James Crawford, Arthur Singleton and I all lived on the same block," Bill said. "They were a little older than I – remember, I had started school early. Anyway, a creek ran behind our houses where we often snuck off to escape our chores and cool down with a swim. Well, we had to have an excuse to tell our parents why we were going off together.

"That morning, my friends called on me at our back door," Bill recounted. "They called me 'Sonny,' back then. 'Hey, Sonny! You ready to go junkin'?' They dragged their burlap bags behind them to make the case that we were going out to work more plausible. As I grabbed my bag and made for the door, Mother said, 'No. He can't go today.' They asked, 'Why is that, Mrs. English?'

"Mother told them, 'Well, we've got a dinner for the church tonight, and I have a bunch of chickens to fry," Lorene explained. "Bill's going to have to kill and pluck those chickens."

Bill was sorely disappointed as he set about wringing eight chicken necks and plunking the carcasses in hot water to loosen the feathers. About 40 minutes into his task, he heard James running through the back yards hollering. "Help, help! George is drowning! Help!"

They later learned that Arthur had stayed at the creek and tried to save George, but the panicking boy fought and kicked so hard that Arthur had to turn him loose. So they ran to his mother's house. By the time they got back to the creek and pulled George out, their friend had drowned.

"The wake was at George's home," Bill said. "To go in that house and see my pal dead in that casket was the first time I experienced death so personally. I was eight years old and it left a terrible mark on me, and others as well. We were all stunned that our friend could be alive and vibrant one day and dead the next."

It wasn't that Bill hadn't seen death, but prior to George's departure, the passing of his elders occurred in a more natural order, like his great-grandmother, Mary Ward.

"Older people died and they were honored in the southern tradition of a New Orleans funeral, with the band marching their remains from the church or wake to the graveyard," Bill explained. "Not everybody had a turnout, but if the deceased had been in an organization like the Elks (that could afford to hire musicians), the service was celebratory. We grieved Great-Grandma, but she was old and had lived a good, long life."

There was no Dixieland Band or pretense of celebration of George's years on Earth. The child was too young. His death was unsettling and unbelievably sad.

Dangerous Liaison
by Bill English

The first time I realized there was something spiritual between my mother and me, I was in Fort Ord, California, for Army basic training. I'd never been to California – it was a big change. I did okay with the rigors of training to fight for my country, but I didn't care for KP (Kitchen Patrol). However, every soldier was expected to take a turn at peeling potatoes and washing pots. The only way out of that odious duty was if a soldier were sick.

One fine day when my name appeared in the kitchen rotation, I claimed illness and the duty sergeant dispatched me to sick bay. There, a nurse took a liking to me. In fact, the woman came on pretty strong, offering me a deal.

"If you want to get out of KP every time you get it, I can give you a pass," she promised. The tradeoff was I had to sleep with her. To me, it seemed like a fair deal, so I took her up on her offer. This arrangement went on for several weeks. Notably, she was White. I was Black. In the early 1950s, this was an extremely dangerous liaison.

Meanwhile, I was in the habit of calling Mother on Saturday mornings. About six weeks into my relationship with the nurse, I called home.

"How you doin', Mom?" I cheerily inquired.

"Before you get into anything, I know what you're up to," Mother said, the worry evident in her voice.

"What are you talking about, Mama?" I replied.

"You're messin' with a White woman," Lorene stated, matter-of-factly. "And you could get killed. Stop it!"

Ever since I was a child, if I attempted fibbing to her, she would deter me with a stern, "Don't even start there, boy. I know you're getting ready to lie." I couldn't lie to her back then and I wasn't about to start that day. But I was flummoxed, wondering, "How in the world did she know this?"

I could tell many more stories about my mother's sixth sense, but this event reinforced that there is a special bond between a Black mother and her first-born son. It wasn't just me. As I've gone through life, I've learned that many of my first-born contemporaries experienced the same thing. Even though they look up to their fathers, they're more their mothers' sons.

In this particular case, Lorene dreamed about my relationship with a White woman and knew her precious son was in dire straits.

Dutifully, I broke things off with the nurse. Not long afterwards, the nurse informed me that her husband was trailing her. It was just a matter of time before we were found out.

I am convinced that I am alive today because of trusting in my mother's dream.

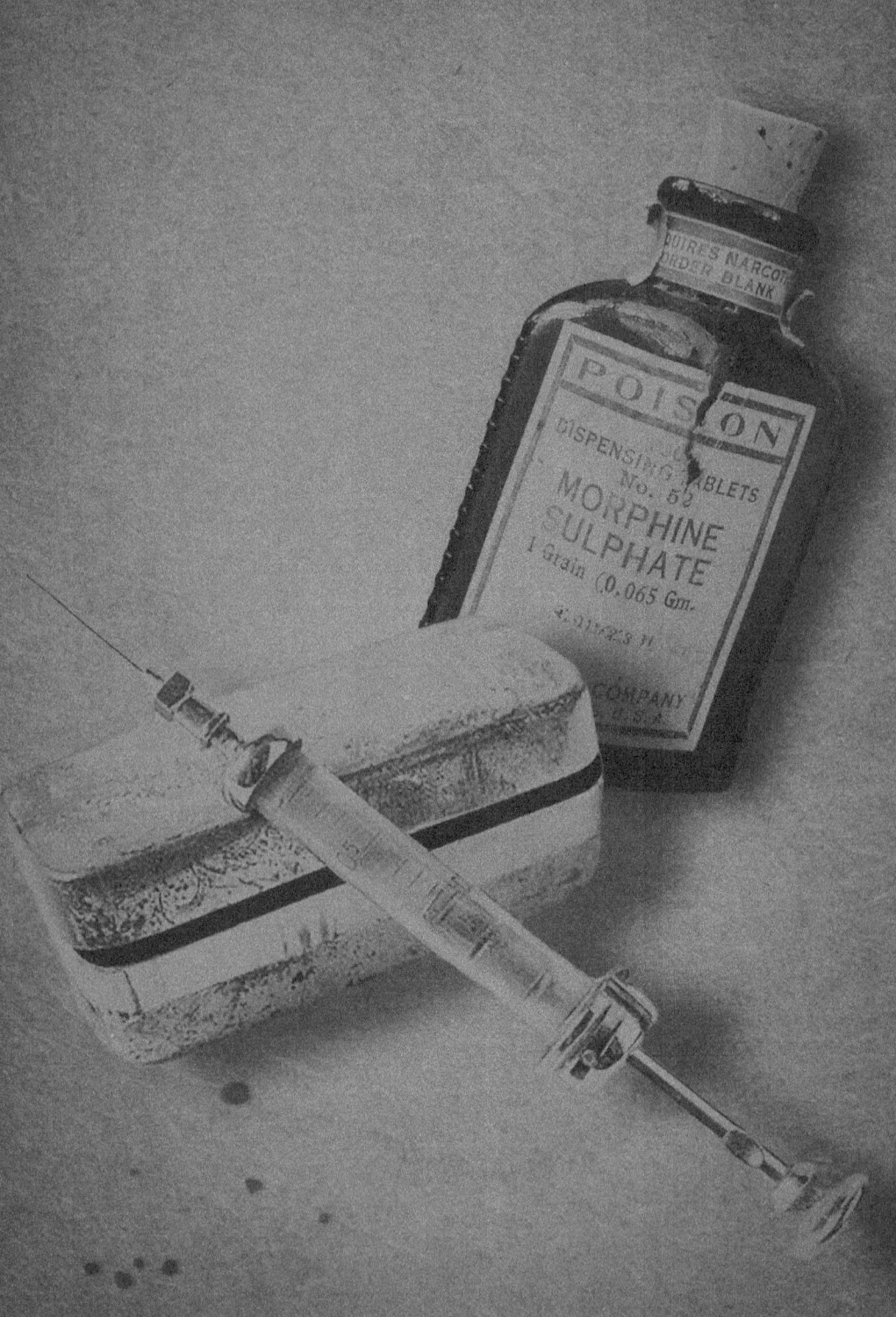

CHAPTER 6
Tragedy at the Steel Mill

Bill's father was horribly injured in an accident at the mill when Bill was 14. He was loading steel onto a truck and was standing between the cab and the bed of the truck to place the big rails into the truck bed. Suddenly, the vehicle moved, his foot slipped and he fell between. But his foot was caught, so the rails kept hitting his head until the operator, finally alerted to the mishap, stopped the loading machine. They pulled the English patriarch out and discovered that the damage was to his head, and it was extremely serious.

"The doctor told my mother, 'He won't last the night.' But defying all odds, although Dad was unconscious, he was still breathing the next morning. Then the doctor said, 'He'll only live a few days.' But my dad was a tough man and he survived. However, his skull and jaw fractures would change him for the rest of his life."

The elder English was admitted to the White hospital in Granite City. The Black hospital was too far away, in St. Louis, Missouri, so the company made a deal with the local institution that if one of their employees, Black or White, was injured on the job, they would be treated locally. They segregated a separate floor for Blacks and Daniel was nearly the only patient on that floor for the entirety of his stay. Others were injured at times, but were only admitted for a few days. Dan, on the other hand, was an inpatient for six months.

"When he came out of the hospital, he was no longer physically or mentally able to work in the steel mill," Bill said, shaking his head.

"When he was sick and his mind compromised during the worst of his convalescence, his employer's legal authorities unconscionably got him to sign off on papers for $2,500 to settle his injury claim. That amount was an insulting pittance and nowhere near touched his medical expenses, nor the staggering loss of income."

Furthermore, and possibly worse than his injuries, the medical so-called professionals gave him morphine every day for six months. He came out of the hospital addicted to the drug, but they didn't give him any more medicine for the pain. The doctors didn't even tell him he had become an addict. They just told him to take some aspirin for his searing, debilitating headaches.

"Later, long past the statute of limitations, Mother checked his hospital records and it was clear he had become addicted to morphine," Bill said angrily. "The racist medical staff knew it. Before his accident, I never saw my father consume more than a half a small bucket of beer with his cronies relaxing over a game of dominoes. But afterwards, he started to drink heavily.

"My mother knew something was wrong with him, because he had never been a drinker, and she made excuses for her husband," Bill said. "'It's that injury,' she'd explain. 'The poor man is in such pain, what else can he do?'"

When Dan was finally well enough to get around, he couldn't go back to his old job. So he bought a used pickup truck and started hauling stuff for people. When folks moved, he was the go-to guy. He'd bring ice to people in the summer and coal in the winter. It was heavy work, yet despite the limitations his accident brought on him, he was determined to support his family.

"When Dad was in the hospital, we were on relief," Bill recalled. "Keep in mind that relief was not something to be proud of, even though a lot of people had to have government assistance of some kind at some time. People could tell the clothing you got for relief was different, so nobody wanted to wear relief clothes. You wouldn't wear them to school because you'd be made fun of. So we only dressed in those relief clothes on weekends and after school. Mom and Dad understood, so they bought us school clothes. The minute we got home, though, off came the good clothes and on went the relief stuff."

The last Joplin lynching

When his father began drinking heavily, Bill lost respect for the man. The 14-year-old didn't understand the excruciating pain his father was experiencing, not to mention the agonizing effects of morphine withdrawal. Instead, Bill only saw the drinking as a character flaw. It wasn't until years later that Bill could look at his father's self-medication with compassion and could feel proud of the man his elder had once been.

"My father experienced events that profoundly influenced his story," Bill said. For instance, Daniel witnessed the last recorded lynching in Joplin, Missouri. That memory haunted him all his days.

Daniel periodically travelled to Missouri to pick cotton. He was skilled at the trade and could pick 300 pounds a day, which meant good money to bring home to his family. They were always so glad to see him walking home at the end of the harvesting season. One time, though, he slouched into the house and dumped all the money he earned on the table. Then he declared, "I'm not ever going back again. That's the last cotton I'm ever gonna pick." Here's why.

After a hard day in the fields, the picking crew sent two of their own to town to buy buckets of beer, which they all drank within reason while they quietly relaxed over Domino boards. They kept to themselves. They didn't want any trouble.

"One night, a couple old pickup trucks rolled into camp and out piled a whole lot of angry, liquored-up White men," Daniel reported. "They grabbed one of our guys, hollering that he'd raped a White woman. But I'm telling you, that man never left the camp. We tried to defend him – we even begged for his life. But there was no reasoning with those boys. They grabbed our friend, tied him up and hung him. I'm not ever going back again, no sir!"

The hanging victim was later found innocent, but it was far too late. At that point, Daniel determined that he would not accept abuse or injustice from anybody, much less the White community.

"I mentioned that we children of the Great Depression era saw our fathers as our heroes," Bill remarked. "Even after his accident and in the throes of alcoholism, he fearlessly defended our family. One time, I saw him stand up to a White man – no small action in the mid-1940s. It made me proud." At the time, White men came around to sell Metropolitan Life burial insurance policies. They'd pick up the small premiums in person every month. This fellow boldly marched onto our porch and hollered, "Lorene?" Daniel, who before his accident hadn't been home during the day, was sitting on the porch, nursing a severe post-injury migraine."

"Who are you?" Daniel irritably demanded.

"I'm the insurance man," the fellow responded, full of self-importance.

"Her name is Mrs. English," Daniel said. "Don't you dare call her anything but that."

Daniel presented as an intimidating figure, standing up to his full height with a crowbar in his hand. In fact, that fellow never walked up on the English porch again. Instead, he stood in the yard when he came by, politely inquiring, "Mrs. English? Are you home?"

"From experiences like that, my father indirectly taught me, 'You don't step off the sidewalk for no White man,'" Bill said. "He meant it and he lived it, even after his brain injury." Despite the pride Bill experienced at Daniel's courage in standing up for Lorene, it was too late to continue looking to his dad as a role model. Bill had already begun shifting hero status to his mother.

"My mother became my champion. She encouraged me to read and write at an early age. She recognized that I was what they called bright, meaning smart. The teachers all praised me, too. But she drove me away from arrogance about my talents, declaring, 'Those are God-given gifts, son. You must be thankful and use them to the best of your ability. In school, nothing less than an A is acceptable.'"

The Metropolitan Life Insurance Company

PART 2

Becoming a Man

"You Owe," Bill's mother told him. "Our people worked hard to create opportunities for you. Now it's your turn. Always remember, you owe."

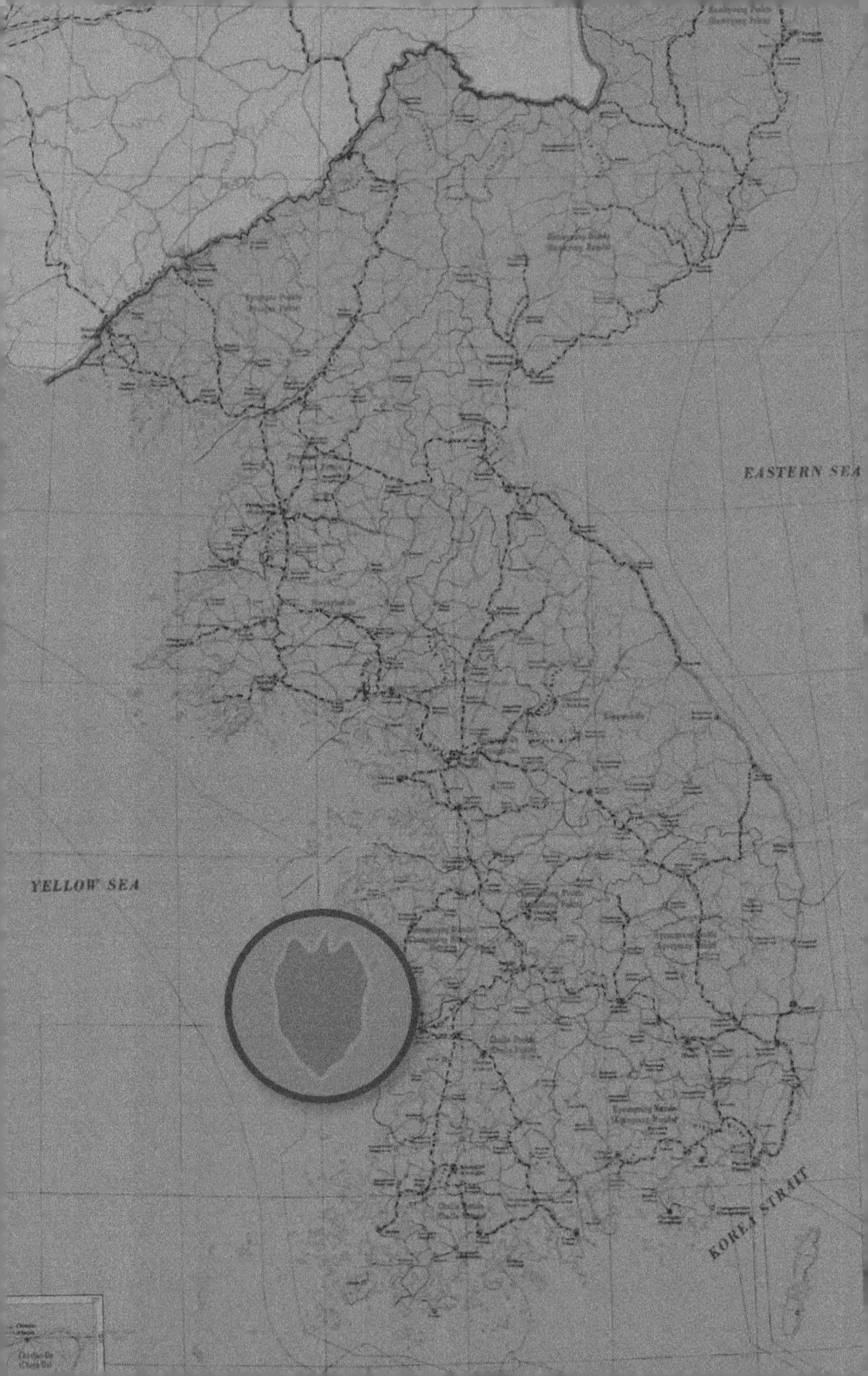

EASTERN SEA

YELLOW SEA

KOREA STRAIT

CHAPTER 7
Army Blues and Academic Hues

"I was drafted into the U.S. Army in 1952 to fight in the Korean 'Conflict,'" Bill said. "They didn't even dignify those hostilities by calling it what it was. It was a war.

"The Army had not fully integrated when I went in, and I never shared quarters with Whites," Bill continued. "In basic training, Black men bunked with Puerto Ricans.

The 24th Infantry Devision, comprised mostly of Black soldiers, was the first to arrive in Korea in the dead of winter. They were not issued proper clothing, weapons and ammunition.

"My cousin was up with the 105th Airborne and lost part of his foot in battle, so they sent him home. My service was in the 105th Artillery Battalion. Another fellow I grew up with went AWOL and was last seen hiding in a cave. He declared he wasn't about to fight without ammo or even proper clothing. He never came home. We figured he was probably captured and killed by the North Koreans.

"What happened in Korea made me ashamed," Bill continued. "I couldn't figure out why we were fighting that war. Because our nation's leaders called it a mere conflict, the American people viewed our fighting as something less than a real war. Yet I saw men dying all around me. Sometimes, I wish that I had the courage to do what Muhammad Ali did, who said NO. I won't be drafted to fight against people I don't know and I have nothing against."

In short, Bill's U.S. Army experience was not good. In fact, it was bewildering, if not downright frightening at times. One positive outcome was when he came home, his military veteran status provided him GI benefits to help underwrite college expenses.

PART 3
Career

Bill's advice to the younger generations is, "First, get an education. Then, find a career you enjoy. Do your job, do it well, work hard. If that means 11 hours a day, so be it. Remember, you owe."

DEDICATED TO
THE OFFICERS AND SOLDIERS
OF THE 82nd AND 65th
UNITED STATES
COLORED INFANTRY

CHAPTER 8
Setting-the-World-Afire Setbacks

"My mother wanted me to be a doctor," Bill recalled. "Of course, there was no family money to send me to medical school. Besides, I didn't like medicine. Maybe because I was so disillusioned by the doctors who supposedly took care of my father and made him into an addict, but that field just wasn't for me. I had to find something else to do. Hard sciences were not in my skill set. Literature, language and writing were my passions. And I wanted to help my people. All markers in my life pointed to social work.

"I earned a scholarship to the historic Lincoln University in Jefferson City, Missouri," Bill continued. "It was a Black institution at the time. In fact, in those days, it was one of two places in Missouri where Black scholars could attain higher education because the state schools were segregated."

Bill packed his few belongings into a cardboard suitcase to head to Jefferson City. But before he could leave, the girl he was dating announced she was pregnant with his child.

Marriage and children

"I met my first wife when we were very young," Bill said. "We were serious and became intimate. I impregnated that girl. Following my mother's rule, I knew I had to marry her and take care of our baby. Well, that set my college plans back for quite a while. I went into the Army and when I returned to the States, I went to work as a parole officer for the Federal Prison in Milan, Michigan. I hated that job – I felt like I was going to jail every day."

The prisoners Bill worked with were not hardened criminals by any means. Many were incarcerated for falsifying information on home mortgage applications.

"Guess what? It didn't come easy for Black folks to get a house

in those states, so they altered their income statements," Bill said. "So what? But that's how authorities incarcerated a lot of Black men. It was wrong."

Eventually, Bill was able to complete a B.S. in Sociology at Eastern Michigan in Ypsilanti. By then, he was divorced.

In 1958, he married a second time. That was when he set his sites on graduate school at the University of Minnesota. Two weeks before Labor Day, he quit his job at the prison, packed up an old station wagon and drove to Minnesota by himself to get established for the later arrival of his wife and young daughter.

"I came to Minneapolis to talk my way into grad school," Bill said. "My goal was to study under Gisela Konopka, a German-Jewish woman and brilliant scholar who had published a book about youth development. She was the recognized expert everybody at that time looked to. When I got here, however, I learned there was no part-time academic option. You either enrolled full-time or you didn't enroll at all. I could have taken extension classes, but that wasn't going to lead me anywhere.

"I called my wife and we came up with the plan that she would support us financially while I attended school," Bill said. "But then, she became pregnant and soon, she couldn't work. I had to find a job, which waylaid graduate school."

Disappointed, but just like his father, always determined to provide for his family, Bill went to work as an underwriter for Group Health Mutual (now Health Partners). The money wasn't very good, but it was a job. Then 3M offered him employment at a much better wage. He was the first Black salesman 3M hired.

Five years later, in the late 1960s, Control Data began romancing him via the St. Paul Urban League. A gentleman named Larry Borom, executive director, St. Paul Urban League, who became Bill's close friend later on, contacted him, saying, "Bill, I've been talking to this new computer company and the applicant they need is you. They want an Equal Employment Opportunity coordinator – someone with social work awareness and business acumen. The money's there and it's a great opportunity. Would you talk to them?"

Dr. Mahmoud El-Kati
"Bill is on the right side of human rights and of history"

Mahmoud El-Kati, educator, activist, lecturer, writer and commentator on the African American experience. Hailing from Georgia, Ohio, Florida and New York, Mahmoud moved to the Twin Cities at age 30.

"When I hit the ground in Minneapolis in 1963, Bill was among the first people I met," Mahmoud said. "We were both passionate about civil rights. The 1960s was a decade that, to some extent, would transform America. In short, things were flying."

He remembers Bill as a passionate yet reasonable young man in a group called Civitas, "Where we had many discussions around questions of citizenship, human rights, race and justice. It was a very informative place for me, talking and listening to people somewhat like me. Bill was one of those people."

Mahmoud is quick to point out that Black people are as complex as any other community in their own way. He contends that they and their leaders don't always get along. In fact, until about a decade ago, when he purchased a lifetime membership in the NAACP, he had a love-hate relationship with the organization.

Despite his differences of opinion with some ideas, overall, he contends that the NAACP is good for democracy.

"Bill and I have crossed paths and been friends and associates over these many long years," Mahmoud said. "I've always known him to be a very responsible person, as engaged as I in the civil rights movement. Of course, we didn't realize we were part of a 'movement' back then. We were simply impassioned about making the world a better place."

Mahmoud was coming at civil rights from an academic's perspective, while Bill was in business. But they both delved deeply into the world of politics as germane to civil rights.

"Like any struggle, you're going to have differences of opinion," Mahmoud explained. "You may agree in principal, but have problems with strategies and tactics with how you get things done. In principal, however, Bill and I were and remain on the same track.

"I was aware Bill was successful at Control Data Corporation, fighting for diversity in the workplace and breaking down senior management race barriers," Mahmoud explained. "I knew him primarily as an activist in our community. I can't possibly count how many activist meetings we've been at together, or protests or picket lines. We've had many discussions with the Minneapolis mayor and city council. It's been a heavy mixture of activity across the board in context with civil rights."

The pair was also part of the KMOJ radio board of directors, a station established to train African Americans about broadcasting and provide communications for the African American community. KMOJ went live in 1976.

"Bill is a good human being," Mahmoud concluded, adding with a smile, "Like all humans – like me – he may be flawed, but he's always trying to do the right thing. As far as I'm concerned, Bill is on the right side of human rights and of history."

Roger Wheeler
Sr. VP, HR and Public Affairs, Control Data Corporation,
1962 to 1984
"That first Black professional in a sea of White faces"

"I'm 89 years old now," Roger reflected as he gazed out the window of his Bloomington, Minnesota office. "A lot of time and events have passed since I worked with Bill. But I remember him and all he did for Control Data." When Bill joined the computer giant, Roger was VP of its worldwide human resources operation, covering 62,000 employees in 47 countries.

"Bill was CDC's first Black professional in a sea of White faces," Roger said. "In many ways, we needed him more than he needed us. You see, although CDC was fantastically successful, we'd come to a point where we needed to add assembly plants. Yet despite all our combined leadership skills, Bill Norris (CDC founder), Norb Berg (deputy chair.) and I knew absolutely nothing about introducing plants into disadvantaged neighborhoods and hiring local talent to staff them in parts of the Twin Cities where jobs were badly needed, but seldom created. We started with the north side of Minneapolis.

"We onboarded Bill not only to help us diversify our workforce, which he most certainly did, but to affect radical change in the way we conducted business internally and externally," Roger continued. "Bill led us into a large minority community and introduced us to people for whom a handful of White executives were heretofore unknown, much less welcomed. Bill was key to our being able to provide 3,000 assembly jobs to North Minneapolis. In fact, that manufacturing facility became the flagship for many such ventures into economically underprivileged cities and small towns across the United States.

"Bill was a go-getter who got things done," Roger said. "He taught us that before we could invite women of color to become assemblers, we had to find a way to provide babysitting for their children. With his vast North Minneapolis network, he knew pastors and churches where we could set up childcare operations." Also, Bill and Roger partnered to help employees with problems unique to the neighborhood. It wasn't uncommon for employees in dire need to reach out to Bill. He, in turn, would contact Roger.

"One time, a woman called with the news that she'd been ousted from her apartment and needed a place to live right away," Roger said. "Nor was it uncommon for somebody needing bailing out of jail. Either he or I would get up in the middle of the night and bring cash to people in trouble. Bill guided us through all that."

According to Roger, among CDC's greatest capabilities was identifying that employee needs in all locations – Black and White alike – were similar. That's why and how CDC created its revolutionary employee assistance programs.

"Every employee population of all races has problems," Roger explained. "CDC's solutions to those problems started with the plant in North Minneapolis, and with Bill English at the forefront. The bottom line is, without Bill, I wouldn't have been welcome among the Black leaders and residents in that neighborhood. Because of him, I was allowed to speak and the locals received what I had to say."

Three key tenets defined and supported the environment in which Bill worked: Norris maintained that profits are like breathing – if you down't have breath, there's nothing else you can accomplish; Companies should pay forward and benefit society for everything that society helped the business accomplish; and Roger noted that Bill broke down many racial barriers with his positive attitude. He led the company into repeating its North Minneapolis success, helping establish facilities in large port cities and small coal-mining towns across the United States and overseas. The only place Bill couldn't go was South Africa, because of Apartheid. Never mind that. Eventually, Bill sat among the highest ranking officers at CDC.

Over time, Bill and Roger became more than professional colleagues.

"We were brothers in Jesus Christ," Roger said. "And we relied on others of similar faith to act on sound employee relations initiatives. He introduced me to Black Christians – I introduced him to White Christians. That first Black professional in a sea of White faces made a huge difference."

Control Data Headquarters rendering, reprinted with permission
from Kraus-Anderson Construction Company archives.

CHAPTER 9
Life-Altering Career Choice

That startup computer company was none other than Control Data Corporation (CDC). Years later, human resources trailblazer Norb Berg remarked, "I was impressed with Bill from the get-go. It's easy to come into any situation as a rabble-rouser and get everybody hot under the collar. But Bill wasn't that way. Sure, he sees the problems. But he also sees answers through collaboration."

Bill took the interview, but after considerable thought, told them, "No. I'm staying at 3M because they've been around a long time and they're not going anywhere. CDC is untried. I have a family to support. I need job security."

Less than a week later, Roger Wheeler, HR VP (who reported to Norb Berg), called him to try to change his mind.

"We got your rejection letter, Mr. English," Roger said. "We hope you'll give us one more chance and talk with us again. We are serious about having you on our team." What Bill didn't know was that Norb Berg, the human resources executive who changed the course of corporate cultures worldwide through his revolutionary and extraordinarily effective employee relations programs, had reviewed Bill's credentials and asserted, "We want Bill English!"

The second interview turned Bill's head. He reconsidered, based on what he perceived was CDC's genuine commitment to integrating non-White staff into their employee retention strategy. He was right.

"I realized 3M was not ready to do anything like that at that point," Bill said. "On the other hand, I believed CDC was ready and willing. They just didn't know how to go about implementing integrated practices."

A staff. A budget. A promise.

"You tell us what you want and we'll make it happen," Roger said. Bill responded, "I require a staff. A budget. And a promise."

"And that's what they gave me. I resigned from 3M and went to work for CDC. It was the best career decision of my life."

That's not to say things were easy. In fact, Bill went to work every day at Control Data (later Ceridian) for 32 years expecting to be fired. Because, "I was never going to accept anything other than first-class citizenship," he said. "And living in a racist country and world, I knew, to borrow an expression from my youth, I would never put my balls in my pocket. I was going to be a man. I knew I couldn't be a White man. I had to be a Black man – the best Black man I could be.

"CDC gave me ample opportunity to make an impact that helped our people," Bill said. "Further, I made a good living. I got a chance to travel all over the world. The company broadened my exposure to a lot of things that developed my realization that business could make a huge social impact if it wanted to. I learned that corporations could have a huge influence on resolving social problems. That's why CDC established plants in inner city areas. That's why they allowed me to set up recruiting efforts in historic Black colleges. That's why they allowed me to make sure that every division had in its personnel department at least one minority who started as a recruiter to learn the business and move up. Those are ideals that Roger Wheeler and Norbert Berg endorsed. Norb, in particular, simply said, 'Yes. We can do that.' Roger and Norb gave me their word. And they never went back on their promises."

CDC leadership rarely said no, because what Bill asked for was not only the fair and right course of action, it was smart business and consistent with the law.

"When I joined CDC, there were precious few minorities around the proverbial company water cooler, there or anywhere in the country," Bill noted. The percentage was negligible. Three decades later, when Bill retired, that number at CDC neared 20-percent.

"We recruited at Black colleges around the country and were able to bring in the best programmers, engineers, computer scientists, accountants and technical writers in the nation – exceptional talent at all levels. The company donated to those universities, as well. It was a two-way street. Organizations like the NAACP and the Urban League welcomed us to have a presence at their conventions. We, in turn, used those events as recruiting tools and a way of advertising Control Data as a great place to work."

Presence

"When I see a problem, I've got to attack it," Bill pointed out. "But there are methods of attack that don't involve hostilities. I learned a much smarter way of doing things. First of all, whether or not I liked capitalism, it was the way to advance our people out of poverty. In my earliest days at Control Data, Walter Leonard – an absolutely brilliant man who was the only assistant ever to serve the former president of Harvard University – advised me about 'mere presence' affecting change.

"One time, I talked with Walter about my apprehensions, telling him, 'Some days, I wonder if I can really make a difference in this company because I'm not going to take any racism from anyone.' You see, I hadn't quite yet come to believe that Control Data was serious about equal employment opportunity. Every day I came into the office, I expected to be fired for something I might say or do. But I learned through Walter that there are critical times when Black people, merely by their presence, can change things. He told me,

'If you listen well and articulate your answers clearly, you can damn sure change things. Remember, even though, as a Black man, you have every right to be angry about society's treatment of our people, blatantly showing your anger isn't always effective. But if you take in your surroundings and practice a little diplomacy, you will make a huge difference. It doesn't mean you have to take crap. But you can quietly assert, 'That's offensive to me. Please, don't say that again. I would never say anything like that to you.' It's amazing how well that can work. "

He did, as Norb Berg explained earlier, get things done through collaboration. But make no mistake – there were times when Bill had to bite his tongue and remember what his mother taught him. She said, "You may not like all White people, but there are good White people. You must always show them respect and demand respect in return."

Bill presents CDC award to Tom Kamp, executive vice president, for his division's achievements in hiring African Americans.

Bill started out as Control Data's Equal Employment Opportunity Coordinator. Then he got to be a manager. Then he was named a director, and after that, promoted to general manager. As the company grew, his staff increased. At one time, he put a sign up at the entry to the HR department that read "Control Data Harlem" as a joke.

"They knew me," Bill laughed. "It was a way of humor. I'd tell White people, 'To enter, you've got to pay tribute. It will cost you two bucks. They'd laugh. But seriously, I knew I was in a highly visible position to role model for all minority employees. It was my job."

Integrating 'Mod A'

"One day, I walked up to the top floor of the old CDC building," Bill recalled. "We called it Mod A – that's where the executives officed. I looked around and there was not one Black face. I remarked, 'You don't even have a Black secretary?' They said, 'Nope. We don't know of any.' I replied, 'I know some.' I went right out and recruited a woman who had been the administrative assistant to the president of the Minneapolis Urban League. I hired her and she became secretary to a vice president at Control Data. They loved her! She was damn good." Further, the woman's professional demeanor

Integrating "Mod A"

demonstrated that it was wise to hire qualified Black women in all aspects of the company. That's when CDC started recruiting at all of the historic Black colleges.

Over time, Bill proved himself so effective that he was promoted to vice president of diversity, a role he held for 17 years. Eventually, he started missing his former career in sales. He had a proven track record as a leader in the organization, and when he expressed interest in moving into sales, he ended up as vice president of Single Source Services, a division that sold engineering repair.

"By the way, I got a chance to travel with Mr. Norris a couple times to testify before Congress," Bill pointed out. "We had markedly different cultural backgrounds, but we respected one another."

CDC provided Bill with a vast array of unique opportunities.

The nation's first affirmative action plan

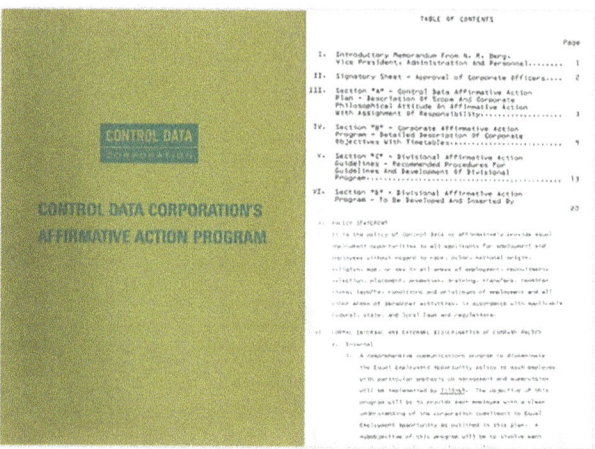

In the early 1970s, Bill English wrote and presented an affirmative action plan to the Control Data executive staff. It was among the first – if not THE first – of its kind in the nation. The company embraced it and in the ensuing years, the concepts laid out in that original plan were intricately woven into the fabric of CDC's culture.

"At one point, CDC made the world's fastest and largest computers," Bill explained. "We pioneered machines aimed at supporting scientists and engineers, so they had to reflect the most robust technology in the market. When IBM claimed to be on the edge of releasing a product that was bigger and faster than CDC's, president and CEO Bill Norris cried 'Foul!' He knew they were nowhere close to the necessary technology. But because of IBM's big name, they had the power to freeze the market. Before they knew what hit 'em, however, Norris slapped them with a lawsuit, proved his case and won, despite Wall Street naysayers." CDC walked away with $1-billion – $500 million of that in cash.

Better to collaborate than compete

"We turned around and bought Commercial Credit, thus giving CDC enormous financial leverage," Bill continued. "After we won the lawsuit, a team from Control Data, including me, flew to IBM Headquarters in New York, where Control Data and IBM began collaborating on computers for a military fighter jet. The point I'm making is this – teaming up underscored that in business, 'There are no permanent enemies – no permanent friends. Only permanent interests.' Those aren't my words, but they are true. It's your interests that motivate you to collaborate. In short, it's better to collaborate than compete. That's how we got things done at Control Data."

The Scam

In the early 1970s, Bill, who was then CDC's equal opportunity employment general manager, started his workday with a review of his daily mail. One day, a slick job-listing periodical grabbed his attention. He looked more closely at the lineup of jobs and the publishing information. Bill thought it looked a bit suspect, so he paid it no mind. Then, the scammers placed an early morning call to Bill Norris. In turn, the CEO asked Norb Berg to look into it. Norb told him, "Fortunately, we have a guy who takes care of Equal Employment Opportunities (EEO). Bill English."

On his next business trip to California, Bill discovered the headquarters turned out to be nothing but a tiny rented space with mailboxes in a Los Angeles strip mall. The people running the scam printed small runs of the "periodical" and claimed their distribution reached and recruited from minority populations across the country. That was a lie. In the end, Bill uncovered a nation-wide scam where Fortune 500 company CEOs were called early in the morning on the basis of pleasing EEO advocates. The CBS news program *60 Minutes* took an interest.

Not long afterwards, Mike Wallace and his television production crew visited Control Data headquarters to talk with Bill. Of course, headquarters was all abuzz with excitement over the interview. The report, entitled *The Scam*, aired in 1974.

"It was a pretty big deal around here," Bill recalled. "But what I didn't realize was that so many friends and relatives all over the country would tune in to *60 Minutes* that night. I should have realized, of course, when I told my mother and aunt about it ahead of time, that they would tell everybody in the world."

It aired. The upshot was the fraudulent owners were put out of business.

South Africa and Control Data

In the late 1960s, Bill and Norb Berg sat down over coffee and began talking about injustice in South Africa. It turned out that Norb had just read about General Motors board member Leon Sullivan's bold stand that General Motors needed to disinvest in South Africa. Norb said, "We should think about that, and what we should do as a company."

Bill responded, "One thing you can do is equalize pay."

That was huge.

According to Bill, Control Data took a stand not only when it made business sense, but also when it was the right thing to do. When the company established a presence in South Africa, CEO William Norris assigned Bill to ensuring that "We would pay Black people the same money as we paid White people. Not only that, we would pay tuition for their kids to go to school.

"Norb Berg backed my work on this 100 percent," Bill said. "The guy is a humanist. He believed apartheid was wrong and wanted to treat all people equally and with respect. In the 1980s, no other company in South Africa was doing that, but we did.

"At Control Data, we didn't believe in anything but equality," Bill continued. "We knew the law. My job was to make sure we were in compliance, and I did my job. Further, we wouldn't pay a woman differently for the same job than what we paid a man. We didn't merely pay lip service to affirmative action – we wrote the book on equal pay."

Time to say goodbye

Over the decades, "Norb protected me from a whole lot of people who wanted him to let me go because they didn't like the way I came at 'em," Bill said." It didn't matter. Norb told my detractors in no uncertain terms that, 'English is getting the job done. He's doing what we want him to do. So if you don't like it, you better let the door hit you in the backside.' Nobody was going to mess with me because Norb had my back and Bill Norris had his."

At the turn of the last century, Bill found things were becoming very different at his place of work. They changed the company name and colleagues with whom he'd cultivated outstanding relationships were leaving. Also, Norb Berg had long since retired.

In 2000, Bill decided to retire. Before he left, he was given a send-off, where invitees were jokingly admonished, "No party poopers!"

Note: In the 1970s, CDC used its considerable influence to get a visa for Rev. Jessie Jackson, Jr., to visit Nelson Mandella in South Africa.

Cyndi Tyner
'Everybody has the same color heart'

"I worked for Bill for more than 10 years at Control Data Corporation," Cyndi said. "I was a single parent with three young children at home and working hard to make ends meet. Bill encouraged me to go back to school. He said I could do my job and attend classes, too – both full time! He was very understanding of the challenges I faced and cooperative with my sometimes wild schedule. He supported my dream and attended my commencement, which made me very proud. He and Freddie gave me a very meaningful graduation gift – a little heart on a chain. I still wear it.

"Bill helped me tremendously as a boss and mentor," Cyndi continued. "He's still in my life as a dear friend. But I wasn't the only one of his staff that he advocated for. He was a teacher to all of us – kind and respectful. Of course, he had high expectations of our professional performance, but at the same time, made it possible for us to create a work environment where we got our jobs done in a pleasurable way."

Bill would coach his team gently, Cyndi pointed out. He was a kind manager, but he wasn't above a little teasing to make his point as long as nobody's feelings were hurt. For instance, "I used to chew gum," she said. "One day, he walked into my office area and told me, 'Never chew gum.' Then he showed me what I looked like when I chewed gum. Well, we had a good laugh and he made his point. Since that day, I have never put another stick of gum in my mouth."

The best memories Cyndi has are how Bill created possibilities for the people who reported to him and really, everybody he came in contact with at CDC. She remarked, "He didn't look at a person for their color – he looked by what was in their heart. 'Everybody has the same color heart,' he told us.

"Bill went above and beyond the expected, too," Cyndi continued. "He stepped into my older son's life, encouraging him as he moved through school and some of the challenges a young Black child growing up in the Twin Cities faced back then.

Note: As Bill recalls, he admonished Cyndi's son, Kevin, to "Get your black ass to college!" Kevin knew Bill meant business and the young man attended college, landed a job in Twin Cities media, eventually moved to California to work with the likes of Jimmy Jam and Jerry Lewis. Among his many professional accomplishments, he established a music magazine.

"Bill and I still talk over the phone and he remains concerned about and interested in me and my kids," she said.

"I loved every bit of my career at CDC," Cyndi concluded. "The truth is that Bill was the best boss I ever had. He mentored by example, and when I began supervising others on affirmative action initiatives, I always aspired to treat them the way Bill treated me."

Cyndi Tyner

CDC Photo Album

If CDC employees were lucky enough to receive this invitation, they were admonished: "No party poopers."

Roy Wilkins, national head of the NAACP, circa 1975

Bill (lower right) with the CDC recruiting team

Bill (far right) and Black CDC employees, mid-1970s

CDC United Way Marathon, 1980s

Roy Wilkins and CDC staffers Glover Martin and Sam Robinson, at a trade show 1970s

Geri Hollingsworth, Cyndi Tyner, Herbert Pearl (a.k.a. "Blood"), who became one of Bill's dearest friends, and Bill. Note the ashtrays in the foreground. Bill kicked the habit of smoking cigarettes, but not before it affected his voice to the point where he could no longer sing in choir. He is adamant that people shouldn't smoke and "kids should never start!"

Leon Sullivan, founder of Opportunities Industrial Center (OIC). Noteably, Mr. Sullivan was the first black person to sit on the General Motors (GM) Board of Directiors. He leveraged that position to pressure GM to discontinue investing in Apartied South Africa.

National Urban League, 1970s: Bill, Vernon Jordan and Jim Beaux

Bill (third from left),
John Calloway (far
right) and CDC
Interns

HUBERT H. HUMPHREY
MINNESOTA

United States Senate
WASHINGTON, D.C. 22510

March 6, 1974

RECEIVED
MAR 8 - 1974
W. E. ENGLISH

Mr. W. E. English
General Manager
Equal Opportunity Planning
Control Data Corporation
8100 34th Avenue South
Minneapolis, Minnesota

Dear Bill:

I understand that you have recently been
promoted to general manager of equal
opportunity planning for Control Data.

I simply wanted to send you a note of
congratulations and to wish you well in
your new position.

Best wishes.

Sincerely,

Hubert H. Humphrey

services

control data institute
**Minority Group
Dynamics
D. G. Wilson/BETHDQ**

Minority Group Dynamics is
a management education seminar that was developed by
Mr. Bill English, Control Data's
Employment Opportunity
Planning Manager. Developed
about four years ago, the
program is designed to assist
our corporation's affirmative
action endeavor by enhancing
management's awareness of (1)
the legal ramifications of Equal
Employment Opportunity
(E.E.O.) Laws and Executive

Bill English

Orders and (2) the vital histori-
cal and contemporary information of the minority groups and
women covered under these
legalities.

The program recognizes that
the standard educational experience fails to include information pertaining to the history, cultural values, attitudes
and consequential actions of
non-majority group members,
and that individuals lacking
this knowledge often have an
adverse effect on organiza-
tional attempts to abide by the
law and implement a program
designed to open opportunities for all of the people.
Control Data Institute Recognizes the value of this seminar
for the management of other
organizations covered under
E.E.O. Law. It is now a part
of the Institute for Advanced
Technology regular course

offering.
Public seminar programs were
conducted in locations such as
Washington, D.C., San Fran-
cisco, Dallas, Texas, and Los
Angeles.

Contracts for this course have
been obtained from the fol-
lowing firms:
• National Bureau of Stan-
  dards
• Dept. of housing & Urban
  Development
• School System—Fairfax,
  Virginia
• School System—St. Paul,
  Minnesota

Information and/or brochures

Cy Bennet

pertaining to this seminar can
be obtained by contacting Don
G. Wilson, BETHDQ (301)
652-2258, Ext. 237.

product services
**Services Bureau
Corporation (SBC) Data
Conversion Capabilities
D. F. Dishinger/SBC**

Services Bureau Corporation
(SBC) presently has two large
scale data conversion centers.
At Birmingham, Alabama, we
have installed some eighty IBM
keypunch/key verify units with
a capability of approximately
16,000 hours per month. At
San Antonio, Texas, we have
installed some sixty (60) units
and are currently generating
some 12,000 hours per month.

The above locations are de-
signated as Data Conversion

CHAPTER 10
The Elephant In the Story

My Four Marriages

by Bill English

Unadulteratedly Separating Fact From Rumor

During my 89 years on this planet, I have been married four times. To maintain authenticity in this book, I strongly feel each of these unions deserves some explanation. Although, I regret many of my behaviors during each of those marriages, I learned much from each wife, and from several extra-marital relationships.

I have prayed for forgiveness from my Lord and Savior and asked for forgiveness from each wife. To those who engaged in my extra-marital relationships, I apologize now for not being as honest as I should have been and although each of you knew I was married, WE WERE WRONG. But as human beings, we are flawed. We were searching for love, but probably in all the wrong places and maybe with the wrong people.

Marriage #1. Phyllis Marie Roberts. We knew each other in our elementary school years. Her father was an associate pastor of our church, Southern Tabernacle Missionary Baptist Church in Lovejoy/Brooklyn, Illinois. When we were pre-teens, her family moved to Springfield, Illinois, about 125 miles from Brooklyn. It was only a 90-minute drive, so we often saw each other during our teens. I'd catch the bus to Springfield, or she'd visit her two older sisters who had stayed in town. Shortly after high school graduation and before my planned first year of college on a merit-based partial scholarship, we were sexually active and she became pregnant.

Upon discovering she was with child, both sets of our parents demanded we marry. Just as my mother admonished me during my early teens, I'd have to "Pay the price for bringing a child into this world."

Neither Phyllis nor I knew anything about love. I was just turning 17 and she was 16. So, the marriage was to placate our parents and legitimize our son, William "Butch" English, with my name on his birth certificate.

I was drafted in 1952 and she was left alone with my military allotment to care for Butch. After my discharge, we realized we did not know each other, had been unfaithful to each other and decided to divorce.

Marriage #2. Jeannie G. Ware. We met in Ypsilanti, Michigan, where I was employed as a parole officer at the Federal Correctional Institute in Milan. Jeannie was a single, beautiful young Black woman with a young daughter named Ramona. Although not my biological child, Ramona was to become my oldest daughter in every way.

During that time, I was taking extension classes from Eastern Michigan University and finished my undergraduate studies through extension and in independent classes. After finding prison work very unsatisfactory, it was clear to me that prisons were not there to rehabilitate, but to incarcerate and use many Black men as cheap labor. I found the federal prison system to be inconsistent with my values. I had promised myself after military service that I would never accept unfair treatment or racism. Without going into details, suffice it to say that racism was rampant in prisons then and continues to this day in most federal and state prisons.

One day in mid-August, 1958, I chose to move to Minneapolis. My intent was to enroll in grad school. We had little savings, and I was hoping that with my part-time employment and Jeannie's willingness to work, we could make it. However, life got in the way and Jeannie became pregnant with Cheryl Denise English, a second child for each of us. Without enough money to care for two children, I had to give up any hope of grad school and took on several jobs.

The best of those was at 3M Companies where I was hired as the first Black salesman.

To be fair, Jeannie wanted and deserved a devoted husband who worked a respectable 9 to 5 job and could build a nuclear Black family with her. Sadly, her needs were inconsistent with my desire to not only work, but really engage in the Civil Rights Movement to the maximum degree.

I jumped into the movement with a fervor and commitment inconsistent with being the kind of husband Jeannie required. My activity in the movement brought me in touch with many of my heroes and many single, beautiful Black women in Minnesota. My vices took over my behavior and I cheated on Jeannie several times. It was shameful and to this day, I regret my unfaithfulness. That cheating led to divorce.

Bill and Cheryl   Ramona and Cheryl

Marriage #3. Shirley J. Hughes. Shirley was a beautiful and talented Black woman who intellectually and physically challenged all my feelings. We became a couple and later married. Shirley chose a professional career and was very good at it. At CDC, she worked for me first and then, when we decided to marry, was promoted to another position at a different site.

We were married for more than a decade and during that time, we shared many fun times. I believe we were truly in love. Shirley taught me a lot, but in very different ways. She was and remains a prolific reader and taught me the joy of sitting quietly on a couch or in my favorite chair listening to jazz or R&B while reading great books. We discussed the events of the day and mostly, shared identical political views.

Shirley and I enjoyed many nice vacations to major cities and the Caribbean. She loved dancing and is a woman of faith. Her family embraced me and treated me very well. However, I am certain I would not have been their first choice for their daughter and sister.

I was not the first to recognize Shirley's brilliance early in her career. She moved up to C-suite senior executive positions at a couple of firms and returned to Ceridian (formerly CDC) as a senior vice president. She earned her corporate success.

Later, we mutually agreed to divorce.

Marriage #4. (four and no more). Freddie Lavern Davis-English: Freddie and I began our relationship during the turbulence of existing relationships with others. She was/is a strikingly beautiful woman with considerable intellect and a serious flair for the fine arts.

Freddie was in the middle of a growing career in the field of criminal justice. She was a fierce professional who demanded equal treatment and respect from her peers. Easy to like and possessed of a great sense of humor, we found that we had many mutual friends.

I have to acknowledge that Freddie used her career to advance other African Americans in the Hennepin County Department of Corrections with her counsel and advocacy. She was promoted to supervisor at the County Home School where her managerial talent was recognized by her superiors. She was later promoted to superintendent of the Juvenile Detention Center, where she was one of a few who achieved equal programing for girls caught up in the juvenile system. She saw the programs established for boys and young men and strongly advocated that girls and young women be given the opportunity through evidenced-based programing to improve their future prospects.

Freddie and I had my youngest and her first biological daughter together, Amber Nicole English. It was an unplanned pregnancy, but Amber has brought us both much joy and continues to impress us and her peers as she has become a committed professional, who is genuinely loyal to her gender and race.

CHAPTER 11
The Fourth Time's the Charm

Bill met and fell in love with Freddie Davis Jones. They wed in 1997 and have been married ever since. In Bill's case, the fourth time is the charm.

"I'd like these pages to reflect the dignity of this woman, who has made my life what it is today," he said. "I want to make sure people see that she carries major influence as a civil rights advocate. There's nobody in the state of Minnesota who has worked harder for women in the criminal justice system than Freddie. She fought for incarcerated females to have the same training, mental health and family support programs as males, particularly in juvenile cases. She informed the powers that be that spending all kinds of money on locking up juvenile delinquents after they commit crimes and not implementing community-based prevention programs was nothing more than barking up the wrong tree.

"Her boss didn't like her outspokenness, nor did that woman much like me, because I was very forward about holding political appointees like her accountable for outcomes," Bill said. "Unfortunately, she couldn't take her anger out on me, so she took it out on Freddie. Still, Freddie always took the high road and stuck to her principles.

"The truth is, our criminal justice system has always been a lot more talk than action and riddled with underlying racism. So often, there were more minority kids and adults in the system than Whites. I asserted the system should be run like a business, and as a business, they needed to produce a product. That product was fewer Blacks being locked up."

Aside from Bill's admiration of Freddie's professional strengths, he is absolutely committed to her as her husband and life partner.

Bill admitted, and then joked, "I kept trying marriage 'til I got it right. But seriously, it was common in my era for a young Black man to act the way I did. It was acceptable. I'm not proud of the mistakes I made, but in the interest of authenticity, I own up to them. Further, I learned a lot from each match and am grateful for the children those women blessed me with."

Bill and Freddie's daughter, Amber, is recognized as a bright and upcoming communications professional with an unlimited future.

"She shares the beauty of her mother and the good looks of her father (tongue-in-cheek) and her two sisters," Bill said. "We raised Amber together and committed to exposing her to all possibilities. That foundation has paid off in many ways.

"As we reach our senior seasons (I am 11 years older than Freddie), we continue to work on improving our marriage and enjoy our trips immensely." Bill said. "With my help, Freddie was sole

caretaker of her aging but smart and funny Tauris Mother, who peacefully passed away at the age of 98. Freddie and I prayed her back to God.

"Freddie is the joy and love of my life who has taught me much," Bill said. "Like other couples, we have endured some pain, but mostly joy. We look forward to any years I have left to combine my full retirement with her passion for the arts and travel."

Bill and Freddie ready for a night on the town. Bill joked that he was going for the *Miami Vice look*.

Freddie and Bill, 2020

Bill maintains he will never forget the first time he laid eyes on the comely Freddie. It was during a convention in Detroit, "And here she comes through the big hall, lookin' like an angel," Bill said with a wide grin. "When I found out she drove a pink Dodge Charger with a white leather top and black and white seats… well, that was that."

Freddie hailed from Tulsa, Oklahoma, but was making her career in the midwest with civic activities. Bill was working with the NAACP. At the time, they were both married to others, so their relationship options were limited. Nevertheless, they had a lot in common and maintained a distant friendship over the phone and running into one another at various events. As time went along and their respective marriages deteriorated, Bill and Freddie became much closer.

"When each of our prior marriages ended, we looked to one another and began dating," Freddie said. "The rest is history." The pair has a daughter together, Amber, who joined them in 1985. But they maintained separate homes until they wed in 1997.

"One of the things that drew me to him was his passion for doing right by his community and fighting for equal justice," Freddie recalled. "I shared that passion. Also, Bill was fun to be with. And, very importantly, we liked the same music – all genres, but jazz in particular. Perhaps most importantly was that he was very much into family. During the course of our early relationship, I got a chance to meet the English family and was impressed by how much they cared about one another. His father had passed by then, but I absolutely loved his mother. They all kind of took to me and took me in."

The wedding party, 1997, for whom Freddie designed and sewed her own and all the females' dresses, and everbody's headgear.

Bill and President Barack Obama at a fundraiser for Amy Klobuchar's campaign.

CHAPTER 12
'Unbought, Unbiased, Unafraid'

"When I was a youngster, an adult Black man was considered someone you wanted to be like," Bill explained. "All of us wanted to be our fathers' sons. But my father's serious work-related injuries sent him reeling into alcoholism and I stopped looking to him to set the example for me. In the most important ways, I was my mother's son. That was good and bad – a double edged-sword.

"When I was a young kid, the men were the heroes in our community," Bill continued. "They ran everything. They owned the business, they were the preachers and principals and town leaders. My generation was the first to become professionals in the White-dominated corporate world. We made great strides for our people and rightfully attained dignity and, yes, pride."

On the other hand, Bill asserts that, for Black people, racial power has shifted. He sees Black men as becoming much more aggressive and utterly unwilling to settle for second class citizenship. That's fair, of course. But today's Black men are also humbled by the fact that Black women are taking their places as real leaders. They no longer walk behind men like they did during the civil rights movement. Instead, they walk side by side or in front of their counterparts.

"Anyway, today I see some slight resentment, but the good news is, we're growing out of it," Bill added. "You can't help but be seriously impressed by people like Stacey Abrams (author, activist, politician and lawyer), Vice President Kamala Harris or so many other Black women of considerable positive notoriety. They're the true leaders that any woman should be. Sure, we're proud of the fact that former President Barack Obama is a Black man, and we watched the leaders of the civil rights movement – like Dr. Martin Luther King, Jr. and so many others. Adam Clayton Powell was my personal hero, but I also remember Shirley Chisholm, who was the first Black woman to run for President. I try to live by her motto – 'Unbought, unbiased, unafraid.'"

Embracing the dynamic gender evolution

"We have experienced and must embrace a dynamic gender evolution, as a culture and a people, to a point now where Black men see their wives as their equals," Bill said. "Why? Number one, females won't tolerate the old ways. Women have asserted, 'We will be seen and heard. We're going to exercise our voices and leadership.'

"Part of that way of thinking emerges from the fact that so many men have been imprisoned for minor offenses, leaving women behind to raise children on their own," he said. "That created generations of female heads of households. We men have seen our mothers, wives and daughters emerging as equals. Today's Black men are much more accepting of the role females have taken. I think we now realize that we are better off because we see each other as equals.

"Dr. King was a giant of a man, but people don't know the women who were behind him. His wife was at the front of the pack, but there were others."

Bill went on to point out the many women who initiated Dr. King's famous March on Washington, where women made all the arrangements, booked the speakers and organized the marchers. They did practically everything, although they didn't get the recognition.

"Let's also consider Rosa Parks, who, after a hard day at work, sparked a revolution with her unwillingness to give up her city bus seat for a White person," Bill said. "She was the catalyst behind the 1955-1956 bus boycott in Montgomery, Alabama, which ignited a powerful economic impetus for civil rights across the United States.

"Moving forward, I'm simply saying that today, I see our race is much better off and our culture will be preserved as much through women as men," Bill said.

Bill English, Freddie English and Barack Obama,
during the latter's first presidential campaign.

Bill "Fitz" Fitzgerald
"I'm proud to be associated with a guy who has more integrity than most people I've met."

"Bill is one of my favorite people," Bill "Fitz" Fitzgerald stated matter-of-factly. Fitz was the VP & GM Computing Devices International US, Ceridian, from 1989 to 1997 and VP Engineering Services at Control Data Corporation from 1985 to 1989. From there, he went to factory motor parts, where he served for a dozen years. He is currently a retired consultant with Insigniam.

In 1973, Fitz was appointed to the role of Control Data Corporation's assistant corporate controller. At the time, Bill English was leading the company's EEO activities. One day, a member of Fitz's staff brought some of Bill's financial reports to him, questioning the validity of Bill's expenditures.

Fitz didn't know anything about Bill. Yet.

"Who is this guy?" Fitz asked. He was told, "Essentially, he's an employee who seems to be playing loose with company funds." When Fitz reviewed the reports, he noted that everything was in order and, indeed, approved by Bill's supervisor. In short, Bill was clearly handling funds with integrity.

The following year, Fitz was promoted to CDC financial plans and controls general manager. In that role, he needed a secretary. When the job opening was announced, Bill showed up at his door asking why there were no Black secretaries on the executive floor.

"I dunno," Fitz replied. "I never even thought about it."

"Well, you should," Bill shot back. "And I have a great candidate for you. Her name is Doreen Rowell and she is eminently qualified." Fitz interviewed Doreen and hired her on the spot. She became the first Black secretary in the company. She proved outstanding at her job. Not long after, coincidentally, Bill and Fitz met on an airplane returning to the Twin Cities from Washington D.C.

"I was surprised when he leaned over to me and said, 'I think I'm going to kill my boss,'" Fitz laughed. "Of course, he wasn't serious. But those words underscored that Bill was very unhappy at work. Fortunately, I needed a salesperson in the international computing division. I recruited him and we worked together very effectively for a long time."

Then came the day that Fitz approached Bill for advice.

"Bill, I have a problem," Fitz explained. "My youngest daughter, Leslie, is five. She had spinal meningitis early on and lost her hearing from it. She's clinically deaf. It's driving me crazy when people mistreat her because of her disability. I simply don't know how to handle discrimination."

"Bill told me to call people on their ignorance," Fitz recounted. "He said, 'When somebody disrespects or makes fun of her, say something to them. You don't have to get mad. Just reasonably explain her situation. Oftentimes, people don't realize they're being ignorant and just need education.'" More times than not, Fitz found that approach worked.

Fitz reports that a single piece of advice launched a lifetime of very close friendship between the two men, and their wives, too. Bill became a second father to Fitz's daughter. He was an advocate for Leslie, encouraging her through her cochlear implants and wearing of hearing aids.

"He danced with her at a family event after her cochlear implant," Fitz fondly recalled. "Today, my daughter has travelled the world over and possesses the courage to stand up for herself in any situation. I give Bill a helluvalotta credit for that."

Bill led a small few who brought civil rights to CDC. Among them was Cora Butler, who in the late 80s, approached Fitz to inquire, "Why doesn't Control Data have a Black History Month?"

"I didn't yet know there was such a thing," Fitz recalled. "So I asked her what she needed to start the program. She said $5,000, some volunteers and support from upper management. So we muscled all that together and initiated Black History Month at the company every February. Because Cora was friends with renowned Twin Cities singer Robert Robertson, she got him to perform at this event several years in a row.

Fitz was flumoxed

"We were having some material losses at the North Minneapolis plant where we built computer cards, a thing of the past nowadays. The cards had no street value except for the very specific computer need. Yet we were coming up short on some of the cards we needed for our clients." Fitz was flummoxed and asked Bill if he thought people were stealing cards.

Bill looked into it and discovered that employees wanted to take the cards home to show their families what they were working on. He came up with the perfect solution: simply throw all the rejected cards into a 55-gallon drum and let people help themselves. The "theft" stopped.

"Bill was a great asset to CDC and me back then," Fitz concluded. "We remain great friends today. I'm proud to be associated with a guy who has more integrity than most people I've met."

Williams
Baudette
International Falls
Island View
VOYAGEURS NAT'L PARK
Wannaska
Karlstad
Middle River
Birchdale
Loman
Pelland
Littlefork
Ray
Gatzke
Newfolden
Grygla
Holt
Thief River Falls
Goodridge
Grand Falls
Big Falls
Waskish
Margie
Crane Lake
SUPERIOR NATIONAL FOREST
BOIS FORTE (NETT LAKE) IND. RES.
RED LAKE INDIAN RESERVATION
Orr
Kelliher
Shooks
Northome
Effie
Cook
Tower
Ely
Plummer
Brooks
Redlake
CHIPPEWA NAT'L FOR.
Togo
Crookston
Erskine
Fertile
McIntosh
Fosston
Clearbrook
Blackduck
Squaw Lake
Marcell
Virginia
Biwabik
Aurora
Winger
Bejou
Bagley
Shevlin
Bemidji
Chisholm
Buhl
Eveleth
WHITE EARTH IND. RES.
Mahnomen
Deer River
Nashwauk
Bovey
Hibbing
Twin Valley
Zerkel
Lake Itasca
Cass Lake
LEECH LAKE IND. RES.
Cohasset
Coleraine
Grand Rapids
Waubun
Ogema
Lake George
Walker
Remer
Swan River
Cotton
Callaway
Akeley
Longville
Hill City
Jacobson
Floodwood
Detroit Lakes
Lake Park
Park Rapids
Hackensack
Backus
Hawley
Menahga
Duluth
Superior
Cloquet
FOND DU LAC IND. RES.
Dunvilla
Frazee
Pine River
Emily
Crosslake
Tamarack
Pelican Rpds.
Perham
Sebeka
Pequot Lakes
Hassman
Cromwell
Barnum
New York Mills
Nisswa
Aitkin
McGregor
Moose Lake
Crosby
Deerwood
Ottertail
Wadena
Staples
Brainerd
Willow River
Fergus Falls
Hewitt
Henning
Motley
Garrison
McGrath
Kerrick
WISCONSIN
ST. CROIX NAT'L SCENIC RIVERWAY
Battle Lake
Eagle Bend
Fort Ripley
Finlayson
Sandstone
Browerville
Little Falls
Isle
Onamia
Hinckley
Evansville
Long Prairie
Elbow Lake
Barrett
Hoffman
Alexandria
Pierz
Mora
Spooner
Osakis
Royalton
Ogilvie
Pine City
Grey Eagle
Sauk Ctr.
Rice
Milaca
Braham
Rush City
Grantsburg
Donnelly
Starbuck
Glenwood
Albany
Sauk Rapids
Foley
Cambridge
Elrosa
Morris
St. Cloud
Princeton
North Branch
Belgrade
St. Joseph
Paynesville
Clearwater
Becker
Zimmerman
Taylors Falls
St. Croix Falls
Cumberland
Benson
Sunburg
Eden Valley
Big Lake
Forest Lake
Barron
New London
Monticello
Elk River
Osceola
Kimball
Anoka
Blaine
Appleton
Milan
Kerkhoven
Spicer
Litchfield
Buffalo
White Bear Lake
Somerset
Dassel
Montrose
Stillwater
Willmar
Delano
St. Paul
Montevideo
Cokato
Baldwin
Minneapolis
Cosmos
Lakeland
Dawson
Granite Falls
Clara City
Hutchinson
Glencoe
Chaska
Spring Valley
Menomonie
Clarkfield
Renville
Olivia
Hector
Shakopee
Savage
Hastings
Ellsworth
Jordan
Farmington
Durand
Minneota
Cottonwood
Vesta
Arlington
Belle Plaine
Hampton
Red Wing
Ivanhoe
Winthrop
Gaylord
Redwood Falls
Marshall
Fairfax
New Prague
Northfield
Cannon Falls
Lake City
Wabasha
Le Sueur
Montgomery
Tyler
Russell
Sleepy Eye
New Ulm
St. Peter
Zumbrota
Kellogg
Tracy
Nicollet
Mankato
Faribault
Kenyon
Zumbro Falls
Florence
Lamberton
Springfield
Waterville
Medford
Pine Island
Plainview
Weaver
L. Crystal
Janesville
Owatonna
Elba
Pipestone
Slayton
Westbrook
Mountain Lake
Madelia
Waseca
Rochester
Lake Wilson
Garden City
Dodge Cen.
Kasson
Hayfield
St. James
Mapleton
Fulda
Windom
Amboy
Blooming Prairie
Stewartville
Chatfield
Truman
Winnebago
Wells
Geneva
Alden
Dexter
Spring Val.
Adrian
Worthington
Jackson
Sherburn
Fairmont
Blue Earth
Albert Lea
Austin
Grand Meadow
Preston
Harmony
I-35W between 3rd St. and exits in Minneapolis is closed for reconstruction until further

CHAPTER 13
The World According to Bill
(and a Few Others)

Bill has well-researched and thought-out opinions. He's reasonable and will respectfully listen to people who don't share his belief system, if they are also respectful. If anybody asks, though, he'll tell them his thoughts on any numbers of subjects. For instance:

Color terms

"Many Black folks avoid the term 'people of color,'" Bill explained. "That's lumping too many people together – Blacks, Hispanics, etc. Today, 'Black' is fine. My mother had to accept being called 'Nigger.' That is a hateful term. It indicates racism at its darkest. When we were kids, if somebody called you Black, you didn't like it. It wasn't until the 1950s that we started understanding that's what we were. We were Black and there's nothing wrong with it. But keep in mind, the only difference between Black and White is the color of the skin. Strip that skin off, everybody's the same. So we accepted the term 'Black.' For my mother, our racial identifier went from variations of 'Negro' to 'colored' to 'Black' to 'African American.' She went through all those name changes and toward the end of her life, still possessed the openness of mind to accept 'African American' as an appropriate identifier for our people."

Justice and guns

Minneapolis was called "Murderapolis" in the middle 1990s. Before she became a senator, Amy Klobuchar delivered a campaign speech addressing killings in the city and focused on locking people up as a tactic toward public safety and crime control. She said nothing about justice. During the Q&A, Bill challenged her, "Tell me where you stand on justice for Black people." She was stunned by that question and kind of fumbled through an answer. Afterwards, she told Bill, "That was the first time I had a question that I wasn't prepared to answer. I'll never be caught that way again. I will always be able to answer from an informed position."

"From then on, when Amy addressed crime, she included equally dispensed justice," Bill remarked. She has come a long way and I really believe in her.

"She's all about sensible gun legislation," Bill continued. "We share a belief in the 2nd Amendment. I simply don't understand why you can't register each gun sold so we can actually track criminals via a serial number. But the gun manufacturers enjoy powerful legislation. Americans have more guns per capita than any other place on the face of the earth. Why in the world do our everyday citizens need automatic weapons?

"In this country, for too long, a lot of the problems are related to guns," Bill asserted. "If we don't get sensible gun legislation, then we're all at fault. We have to look in the mirror. We tolerate the NRA dominating the land, while almost 70% of Americans believe in reasonable gun control. I, for one, was so glad to hear President Biden promise to ban AR-15s. Unfortunately, that ban lapsed.

"Politically, I'm a progressive. The truth is, what's being allowed today is seriously jeopardizing our democracy." However, Bill went on to assert that America has taken great strides since the days when the content of one's character mattered far less than the color of his or her skin.

"As a society, our country continues to evolve," he explained. "The struggle to find a perfect union continues. We are on the verge of civil war. It's scary."

Gangs

"From a social perspective, let's consider how drugs were introduced to the Black community," Bill explained. "First of all, we have to look at the Iran-Contra affair and Ronald Reagan. When the U.S. government used cocaine to fund the Contras, in essence, Reagan's CIA agents introduced cocaine into the African American community. It started in South Central Los Angeles and quickly spread across the country because there was so much money to be made. The real money and power was with unscrupulous White men who bought the drugs and distributed that poison to local dealers, who were primarily young Black men."

One Saturday morning as Bill waited his turn at the local barbershop, he sat listening to the wisdom of his elders. One wizened fellow leaned over to him and stated, "We don't own no planes, boats, trains or over-the-road trucks. So who brings drugs into our community? Just think about that. It's the government."

"Drugs became a way in which young Black men could make a lot of money," Bill said. "They took all the risk. And so drug turf became a way of fighting over drug money. There's a semi-biographical movie depicting the life of the *King of Harlem* – Bumpy Johnson – a huge drug dealer. Matter of fact, he helped finance several of Malcolm X's initiatives. That dealer co-existed with the police in Harlem – he paid off the authorities and they allowed him to operate. We're talking huge bucks in that case."

Poverty is multi-racial

Bill continues to speak out against criminalizing drugs in marginalized communities and he isn't limiting his statements to Black areas. For instance, "When Control Data built facilities in Ohio and Kentucky, they had huge meth and poverty problems," he said. "Authorities in those regions thought of low income miners as hillbillies. That's just wrong. White men were dying from black lung disease and the government was ignoring it. The mine owners were making huge dividends – 'grand theft money,' as it was known. That's when I, with Control Data's backing, went in with plans to genuinely affect change in those communities.

"It was then when I began to realize why Dr. Martin Luther King was killed," Bill said. When he started talking about the *Poor People's March* on Washington and bringing Black, White and Brown poor people together, the powers that be dictated he had to die. James Earl Ray is associated with King's murder, but no one claims to know how Ray escaped and traveled to Europe. J. Edgar Hoover called Dr. King the most dangerous man in America. No sooner was the civil rights leader murdered than Hoover switched his attention to Malcolm X, calling him the most dangerous man in America. Two prominent Black leaders were assassinated. I don't get into conspiracy theories because they're just not healthy. I'm fact-driven. On the other hand, the facts surrounding those deaths are pretty dicey."

Politics and policies

Bill believes capitalism is an answer to the U.S. economic problems. Published in 1946, *The Capitalist Manifesto*, states his case. Written by an attorney and economist, the book's premise is this: If the The United States government declared that when a certain level of multi-millionaires died, their estates would be required to pass a percentage of their wealth to the government. That would lessen the tax burden on everyday citizens and empower everybody to become a capitalist.

"Jeff Bezos, one of the richest people in the world, doesn't pay a dime in income taxes," Bill noted. "On the other hand, Warren Buffet, another very wealthy man, asserts, 'It's wrong for my secretary to pay more in taxes than I do.' Buffet's principles reflect mine. We could solve our poverty problems in a New York Minute if we'd fairly tax the super-wealthy. Unfortunately, our government is controlled by a very wealthy cabinet which favors tax breaks for its contemporaries."

Healthcare

"We are the wealthiest country on the face of the Earth," Bill said. "Yet people die every day because they don't have healthcare insurance. What's wrong with us? In Canada, for instance, you get appendicitis, you get surgery and you walk out with no bill. We, on the other hand, pay through the nose. Another problem is pharmaceuticals. We're still trying to find the cure for diabetes.

Meanwhile, medicine to treat it costs so much that patients cut their insulin use in half."

Bill pointed to the Barack Obama presidential campaign promise to cut down on astronomical medical care costs. As president, he was as good as his word through the Affordable Care Act, which covered 44 million people. That makes a lot of sense to me."

Community leadership and service

In 2005, hundreds of people, businesses and organizations whom Bill English positively influenced over the years organized a celebration of his decades of community leadership and service. The following event program excerpts offer insight into his deep impact on many individuals and programs.

Tim Baylor
"Bill is like family"

Tim Baylor came to town from the Baltimore Colts to play with the Minnesota Vikings in 1979. After retiring from the field, Tim became an important major business developer.

"One of my high school teammates from Washington D.C. introduced us," Tim said. "Bill invited me over for a cookout and began introducing me to people he knew. In fact, he arranged for my wife to get a job at CDC. That's how it all got started. We've been friends since then – no fallings out. I've helped him at times, but more so, he's helped me with his wisdom, insight and extensive network of contacts locally and nationally."

Over the years, as Tim transitioned away from football, he and his wife decided to stay in the Twin Cities and raise their young family. Bill continued to make business connections for Tim and when the younger man ran for governor of the State of Minnesota in 2006, Bill supported him.

"I had no experience in politics, nor did I really like politics," Tim said. "I had no idea how it all worked. Bill was instrumental in showing me the landscape and teaching me about political processes." Bill encouraged Tim when and how to speak with other politicians in the community, too. Tim didn't win the race, but, "I don't know how I would have done without Bill's guidance and political acumen. He was like a personal consultant – somebody I could trust and rely on when things got tough. And believe me, things did get tough. Politics is a whole different world."

Tim says that Bill English is family to him. During the Obama inauguration, they were together in Washington D.C., where the English family stayed at the Baylor home.

Tim enjoys it when Bill talks about his upbringing, noting, "He is the oldest of 13 kids. Typically, older kids take on a lot of responsibility for the younger ones. It's clear he's been responsible for others most of his life. He came from humble beginnings. Like many of us, he ascended and broke the glass ceiling in the corporate world, achieving the executive leadership level, which wasn't popular in a Fortune 500 company back then. And he did it with aplomb, always reaching back, to this day, to pick somebody up and give them encouragement."

Tim's favorite memory with Bill happened at the State Democratic Convention in Rochester, Minnesota.

"The way he supported me and the way I saw him matriculating through the system, getting things done and conveying that back to me was masterful," Tim said.

"I just saw him at a 4th of July [2023] gathering," Tim continued. "He is a very stylish and savvy dresser. At 89 years old, he's in better physical condition than a lot of people my age [Tim is 20 years younger than Bill]. His mental acuity is all there." When the two of them sit down together, their age difference is of no matter.

"Age doesn't factor into the respect and love we have toward each other," Tim stated, matter-of-factly, adding that when a person is smart, which Bill definitely is, wisdom comes with age.

"I grew up with the JFK and Martin Luther King assassinations," Tim said. "I came up traveling with my dad and having to drink from the colored water fountains. I can relate to those things. Bill's core knowledge, experience and history, on the other hand, reaches back even further, into the Jim Crow era. He has amazing political perspective to share when young people try governing today. He helps them put today's events into context with history.

"People should know, if they don't already, that Bill never met a microphone he didn't like," Tim added with a laugh. "And when you give him the mic, you have to be ready to take it away from him. Because he likes to expound on things he cares about. Very importantly, Bill has no problem with speaking truth to power. My interpretation of 'truth to power' means that Bill will not be intimidated by your position in society or the amount of wealth you may have obtained. His candor is unfiltered! In my experience, he will not be compromised by others. He takes a position, and may not be right all the time, in my opinion. But he's passionate about his perspectives and will defend them – defend **you** – to the end.

"Bill is not the first great Black Minnesotan," Tim said. "But he's one of the greatest I know personally."

Andrea Jenkins
"Show up, be present and be part of the conversation"

Andrea Jenkins is a Minnesota politician, public servant, writer, performance artist, poet and transgender activist. She has served on the Minneapolis City Council since January, 2018, and became the Council's president two years later. She is the United States' first openly transgender Black woman elected to public office. Andrea is also Bill's friend.

She was in her early 20s when her uncle, who was a good friend of Bill's thought the two should meet. Over the decades, "I've mostly related to Bill as a friend, but our paths have crossed in public service," Andrea stated. "Bill is a community leader and advocate – I'm a council member. We work on various projects together. He chairs the board of the Sabathani Community Center, located in Ward 8, which I represent."

"'Sabathani' is a Swahili word," Andrea explained. "Since Bill helped found it in 1966, the organization has provided vital services to help community members find jobs and access to clothing and food shelves. Also, therein are vital youth and senior support services, not to mention the space rented to various community organizations that provide a broad array of community services."

In a word, Andrea would describe Bill as "passionate." But according to her, one word cannot possibly sum up his work for African American rights and the community at large.

"When we first met, he was a business executive at Control Data Corporation," Andrea said. "He was very professional then and remains that way. And his commitment to Black rights wavered one bit.

"Bill has a keen sense of history," she continued. "He holds a tremendous amount of knowledge around community development and the folks who have contributed to making this city. He is extremely politically engaged, having fostered relationships with senators, governors, state representatives and council members. He's intricately connected in that realm."

Very importantly, Andrea noted, Bill holds elected officials accountable and can be very pointed in his criticism of those who don't fulfill what he considers their responsibility to their constituencies.

"Bill English is a committed public servant who cares deeply about the Black community and is always willing to bring his talent, skills and expertise toward building a better community. He has had a significant impact on race relations in the city of Minneapolis, for sure. He's been a positive force in a number of projects designed to help build development and economic wealth in communities.

"Bill has shown me what it means to show up, be present and be part of the conversation. That has been his impact on me – to be willing to speak up when things are happening, but to also be pragmatic – strategic – in how we approach issues."

Bernadeia Johnson
"Bill speaks truth to power"

Bernadeia Johnson is an Educational Leadership professor at Minnesota State University. As the former Superintendent of Minneapolis Public Schools, school principal, administrator and student advocate, she is eminently qualified to teach the subject. She worked with Bill over the course of five decades.

Bernadeia grew up in Selma, Alabama, and began her career in Minneapolis after graduating from the historically all-Black college of Alabama A&M University in 1981. Twenty-three years later, when she became an academic officer in the Minneapolis Public School District, she crossed paths with Bill English for the first time. Her professional life was changed forever, for the better, "Most of the time," she laughed. "Bill called to set up a face-to-face meeting. He's like that. He wants to be sure to make the connection.

"My first impression was that he wasn't leaving anything to chance," she said. "He wanted me to know who he was, what he stood for, what he thought of the system and what we could do to improve it. We've been friends ever since."

Bernadeia and Bill saw eye to eye on the need and urgency to take action on behalf of Minneapolis school students. There was too much at stake – too many young lives to be redirected.

"He wasn't exactly proposing a strategy," she said. "At the time, I was the chief academic officer and not yet taking on superintendent duties. My sphere of influence was exclusively in curriculum development. Bill wanted to ensure I was capable of and competent to do the work I needed to do.

"Bill is an individual of gravitas," Bernadeia reflected. "He's smart – not just intellectually, but street smart, too. He possesses the kind of acumen that allows him to quickly grasp issues. He also speaks truth to power – he's not afraid to talk about what he knows, and learn what he doesn't know. If you're able to just listen to him and ask questions, he'll work with you to understand and address complex issues."

Bernadeia further noted that Bill can be an adversarial advocate. In fact, she said, he cares so much that he will challenge anything and everything to ensure the cause he's fighting for has addressed a topic from all possible angles. Yet as thorough as he is, Bill doesn't use a lot of extraneous words. He cuts straight to the chase.

"Bill is an authority figure to me – kind of like a father," she said, adding with a smile, "though sometimes I fear he thinks I'm a little naive. For instance, when he helps me prepare for a meeting, he makes sure he 'schools' me on the dynamics of the group and how different people are going to act. He insists I strive to be the best version of myself, showing what I know and demonstrating my authority around an issue. I'm often the only professional educator around the table and certainly the only former superintendent. He'll advise me, 'You are in this position for a reason. I'm here to remind you of that and want you to act as such.'"

Bernadeia addressed Bill's interaction with young people, explaining that Minnesota statute directs that students who are behind academically for their grade levels and not doing well in regular public school should have access to contract alternative learning programs.

"Bill ran one of those for me," she said. "It was called 'The City Inc. Alternative High School.' He proved that we could take the worst students in our district – the kids Minneapolis schools discarded – and help them become productive citizens. Bill was critical in building up his students' self-esteem and making them believe in themselves. He and his staff helped many, many students – kids who heretofore may have been headed for a life of poverty and crime – earn their high school diplomas and get on track for college."

Bernadia always enjoys Bill's sense of humor. The two of them still laugh a lot when they get together.

"I tried to keep my composure at board meetings, but I can't deny that I thought it was funny when he would come and light the board up. He'd just lay his fruit on the table and they'd be all uncomfortable with his directness. You see, Bill

wanted everything to be transparent – not take things offline in private conferences. And Bill knew how to move his ideas forward. Sometimes he came loaded for bear. He was always ready for conflict, but rarely let things go too far. That is where his Control Data work and business acumen truly shone."

Josie Johnson
"He was quite willing to speak the mind of many toward justice and equality"

"We've know each other forever," Josie Johnson said of her friend, Bill English. Josie is a retired University of Minnesota professor. She resides in Minneapolis, where she has been a tireless equal rights advocate since the 1950s. Her memoir, *Hope in the Struggle*, opens with the following statement, which makes it clear why and how she and Bill English have occupied the same social justice space for decades:

> *For the ancestors who struggled for me*
> *For the future generations for whom I struggle*
> *Always in love and always for justice*

"Bill is like a little brother to me," Josie stated. "We met way back in the 1950s, when we were all active politically in our communities. Bill was with me and among all of us who worked hard visiting legislators and preparing legislation toward equality and justice."

Josie grew up in Texas and came to Minneapolis in 1956 to be active in the civil rights movement, engaged with Democratic Governor Orville Freeman and fight for "whatever was of value to our people, like fair housing legislation and other glaring issues of that period. I was a lobbyist, activist and what some might have called an all around troublemaker," she said, with a smile. "I'm pleased to report that Bill was a troublemaker right along with me at public demonstrations and formal meetings alike. I loved what we were trying to do. And I believe history will say that we were successful in gaining much needed housing and job opportunity legislation. We stayed on top of those issues for the Black community.

"I have proudly watched Bill over many decades as he has worked in the community trying to improve things for our people," Josie continued. "In my judgement, he is a well-educated, well-informed person who is very interested in and committed to his community. He was one of the people you could always depend on to speak out honestly and oftentimes forcefully about issues of equality, as we were all fighting for. We looked to him to be consistent and articulate about the issues without fear or hesitation. He was quite willing to speak the mind of many toward justice and equality."

BILL ENGLISH ALWAYS
LOOKS LIKE A MILLION DOLLARS

Written by Rose McGee

A Tribute to William "Bill" English – June 14, 2008

Rose McGee founded the Twin Cities Sweet Potato Comfort Pie, an organization "which advances racial justice, heals damage from race-based trauma, and elevates marginalized voices." Bill notes that Rose is "a brilliant and engaged servant leader."

Bill English
>   always
> looks like a million dollars
>   wearing those striking tailored suits
> and spit-polished shinny shoes
>   but he's deeper, much deeper than that
> even though he naturally knows how
>   to move with a jazzy groove in his strut
> that only a *Brotha* can pull off especially
>   on days when Capitol Hill blues
> or institutional racism attacks and tries
>   to take hold wanting to loop
> Bill's handsome designer tie into a noose
>   around his own neck then stage a lynching
> exhibition by a system that has often said,
>   "You listen! Enough is enough – so get back!"
> Not this man – who for decades continued
>   to withstand troubled waters of realities
> that made him not only want – but DID holla back
>   at a broken-down system,
> "Nawh! You listen! Enough is enough
>   I ain't turning back! Nawh!"

Bill English...
>   always
looks like a million dollars
>   whether posing for a Tobechi destined
award-winning photo that lured thousands into
>   picking up an *INSIGHT* to read and understand
what defines a man
as being a servant, a civil rights
>   mover and shaker right here in our own midst
one you don't want to mistake as being anything other
>   than what he is – the wind beneath many wings
including
countless teens and beings who
>   have yet to even meet the man because...
he is an individual who has paid his dues –
>   McCain! Listen up – ARMED FORCES?
Bill's been there and done that too
>   Donald Trump! WHERE YOU AT?
English knows when a preposition's
>   out of place, but on a slightly different *set*
he used to ask, "Where my boys at?"
>   cauz they were NOT in the corporate board room
where he often sat alone fending for himself
>   yet when time came around he was taking
time to listen to "the people" of all nations, populations,
>   denominations, education, reputations,
desperations, limitations
guiding them through mediation, hesitations onto
>   determination, innovations, dedication which
created even greater
aspirations, motivations undertaking
>   OBAMA
destination only because leaders like English
>   helped pave the way for this amazing
history-making situation.

PART 4
Community Elder

After decades of serving as a positive force in north Minneapolis and beyond, Bill is now considered an elder in his community. But he is never one to rest on his laurels. He continues to be an inspiration to young people, advise businesses, stand for justice, promote industry in the neighborhood, and hold politicians to their promises.

Bill in October 2023 at the former CDC plant in North Minneapolis. The building is now a school.

CHAPTER 14
Passing the Baton

When the sun sets on one generation, it rises on another.

Clockwise: Freddie, Ramona, Cheryl, Bill and Amber, early 1990s

As a man born in the 1930s, Bill knows his number of years left on the planet are statistically few. How does he feel about moving into elder status?

"It's the way of life," Bill reflected. "Nobody gets to live forever. Yet I believe that a person's legacy lives on in his or her progeny. My children and their children carry on the lessons I learned from my parents, and their parents, etc."

Bill is, without a doubt, a family man. He cares deeply for his wife, children and extended family.

Amber, Ramona, Butch and Cheryl, circa 2007

As did Bill, some of his children reflect his parents' characteristics. For instance, he says his middle daughter has his father's steadfast work ethic. The other daughters show signs of his mother's powerful personality. Also, any one of them is ready to take charge at a moment's notice.

"All of my kids possess an inherent curiosity and stand on principle," he said. "I love them dearly and am proud of each and every one of them." His three surviving children offer unique perspective into the man who is to some, a legend. But to them, he is simply "Dad."

Ramona English, daughter #1

Born in 1953, Ramona is the eldest of Bill's daughters, and by her own admission, is far and away the most quiet. Bill helped raise Ramona from the time she was in kindergarten.

"My next sister, Cheryl, was always out and about with Dad – he was a force to be reckoned with in the community and she could keep up with him," Ramona smiled. "I just wasn't interested in meeting and being with all those people." But Ramona was no shrinking violet. She stood and stands solidly on her own.

"Dad was always a mainstay in the community – if you were new in town and needed a job, you were told to contact Bill English," she said. "If you had been in town all your life and needed a job, you were told to contact Bill English. If you needed advice or guidance on how to handle disparity or discrimination, you were told to contact Bill English."

Furthermore, "Dad doesn't meet any strangers," she said. "He talks with everybody. He's extremely knowledgeable and is always trying to help out others. I remember growing up and hearing the kids a few years older than me saying, 'Your dad got me my first job.' Everybody knew who he was, to the point that I'd introduce myself and they'd say, 'Oh, you're Bill English's daughter.' Boys my age would react with, 'YOU'RE Bill English's daughter,' and then wouldn't talk with me because they didn't want to get in trouble.

"My name is English," she said. "I'm proud of my family heritage, but I am my own person."

Ramona was just starting school when Bill and her mother moved from Michigan to Minnesota. She has fond memories of him teaching her to ride a bicycle. He'd given her a regular bike with no training wheels. The pair went outside one afternoon, he showed her the basics, lifted her onto the seat and told her to start pedaling.

"I was a little nervous, but he stayed right behind me until I got the hang of it," she recalled. "It's like he was as a dad – there when I needed him."

Both parents were pretty strict with her, which she didn't really mind because she was a good kid. She was smart and very athletically talented. An athlete himself, Bill supported her life of track and basketball. She ran every morning, no matter the season. Her dad was very proud of her sports accomplishments. Whenever he could, he was on the sidelines cheering for her.

Ramona didn't get especially close to her grandmother, Lorene, but remembers visiting her in East Saint Louis, which was "A world away from my life in Minnesota. But it was fun for me because there were so many aunts and uncles and other kids around to play with."

Ramona was aware that her dad worked in civil rights and had a sense of how much others respected him. She heard him speak at different events and at home, where, "People would come by for various meetings. I would hear their conversations, but you know how kids are – I didn't really engage in the older generation's discussions. Still, I knew they were talking about important subjects."

Eventually, Ramona settled in Texas to pursue a career in banking. She recently retired from that to open her own fitness training business. She is a woman of faith and has served in leadership positions for several non profit organizations.

"I am happy to say that Dad took a true interest in both my sons, Cliff and Joshua," she said. "He has been active with them all their lives."

Cheryl English, daughter # 2

Cheryl came on the scene in 1959. Her earliest memories include watching her dad fly out the door, headed for work. Also, "I remember reading the paper with him on Sundays. That was always important. From a very early age, before I could actually read the words, he'd read aloud to me out of the paper. I got my love of reading and keeping up with the news from my dad."

Although her parents divorced when she was 11, "Both raised me," she said. "Dad stayed very active in my life. Trust me. Very active. He always seemed to know what I was up to.

"He was a no nonsense dad," she said, matter-of-factly. "When you came home from school, you sat down with homework. You didn't go outside to play until you finished. If it wasn't done, somehow, he'd know. He'd call from his office to check.

"In the summer, he didn't mess around, either," Cheryl continued. "He called the television set *The Idiot Box*. He'd roll his eyes and demand, 'You're not going to sit and watch that idiot box all day.' We were expected to get up and do something. We had to finish our chores and go outside. Granted, there wasn't much on T.V. back then, but the point was, we had to get up and go."

Bill's second daughter was interested in his civil rights work from the get-go. From first grade on, Cheryl tagged along with him whenever she was allowed to. After she was a little older, she accompanied him to national political rallies in Washington D.C., Urban League conventions in California, Control Data recruiting trade shows in New Orleans and local marches, like down Minneapolis's Hennepin Avenue through Loring Park.

"My father was a combination of strict disciplinarian and fun dad," she said. "We'd go on the rides at Excelsior, which is now Valleyfair, and he took us to Como Zoo. We went on family vacations to the lake, too. And how he loved Christmas, always insisting on a 'real' tree. He'd watch each and every one of us open our gifts in the morning and then we'd have a big festive dinner. But as I said, he was very strict. I think he just wanted us kids to live up to our potential."

Cheryl's admiration for her Grandma Lorene is clear.

"She was a very strong woman who didn't take any nonsense," Cheryl said with pride. "I spent some summers down in East St. Louis with her, along with other cousins. She raised her kids right. Nobody was jealous – nobody turned out to be a criminal. All had successful careers. She was employed well into her 80s. Her work ethic was non-stop.

"Grandma was a deeply religious person," Cheryl pointed out. "The only time you could miss church was if you had to work. If you're on your deathbed, you're going to church. No excuse. But if you said, 'I have to work,' you were given a pass."

Partially following in her father's footsteps, Cheryl grew up to work in corrections. This mother of one grown son spent 30 years working with children, starting at the first African American group

home for juvenile males, a major step forward in the early 1980s. She then was employed by Hennepin County's Home School-Residential Treatment Center, and later, returned to counseling juveniles at risk until she went to work for the Minneapolis Public Schools. She is semi-retired nowadays.

"I learned from both my grandmother and my dad that everyone deserves a second chance," Cheryl said. "Sometimes those kids were just thrown away. That's not right. Everyone deserves a fair shake."

Lorene English, 2000

Cheryl credits her commitment to fairness to her father, who taught her to always stand up for what she believes. She notes, "In certain situations, I didn't back down. I definitely got that from him. I can't describe how important he's been in my life. He is my best friend."

Bill noted, "Cheryl was always a champion of the underdog. When she was in school, she often brought home children who were bullied and insisted that her friends accept these kids as their friends, too. As an adult, she adopted one-year-old Jabraun and raised him. Although somewhat challenged, he has grown into a wonderful young man who proudly serves as an assistant teacher in the Minneapolis Public Schools, where he has received several awards for his performance and dedication to students."

Amber English, daughter #3

In August of 1985, along came the baby of the family, Amber. Today, she is the communications director for Congress Member Nikema Williams of Georgia's 5th District. She spends her days writing speeches, managing social media, writing copy, taking pictures and planning events. She started her life, however, feeling like there was a lot to live up to, noting, "There's such an age gap between me and my sisters that for a long time, they were more like aunts to me. I grew up as an only child."

Her earliest memories of her dad include him taking her to various stores to pick up things she needed.

"He did not like shopping, but he would take me to Southdale, to Daytons to buy clothes or Stride Rite to get my shoes," she said. "Of all things, he was adamant about getting the car washed every weekend. I would ride with him to the car wash and then go to the cleaners. Dad is serious about being a sharp dresser and maintaining his wardrobe. So we would go to One Hour Martinizing, run errands and go back to get the clean clothes. That was our Saturday ritual.

"I grew up in a very unapologetically Black and proud home," Amber said. "I knew my grandmother – we called her 'Lobie.' She was definitely stern. I think she's where Dad got his strict ways and focus on academic success. His thing was, 'I know what you're capable of.' One time in high school, I was enrolled in AP European History. I just didn't want to take that class. I really wanted to take world history. But at my school, that was considered a basic class. Not AP. If you wanted honors or AP, you were required to take European history. That seems kind of backwards to me now, but anyway, I wanted to drop the class. Dad didn't want me to. He LIKES European history. That was a real source of frustration, but sometimes, parents wanting us to succeed doesn't always translate into the kid's preferences.

"My dad is certainly where I got my career path," Amber said. "I learned from him to never be afraid to call things as you see them. In my senior year, we had a class called "Modern Problems," where we talked about things that were happening in the news. One time, there was something serious happening at the state capitol. My dad and some republican legislator exchanged words and Dad uncharacteristically pointed in his face and yelled, 'You're a redneck!' The exchange made the news. The next day, I went to school and in class, the teacher brought up this incident. He mentioned 'Bill English' and the whole class looked at me.

"'Yeah, that's my dad,' I said. "Mmm hmmm. I'm very familiar with what happened at the state capitol yesterday.' I didn't necessarily feel embarrassed by it. I had my own qualms about how Wayzata High school handled racial differences. That high school was not a Black school by any means. It was quite an experience for me. My classmates had acceptance issues. At the time, legislators dictated that Minneapolis public schools had to bus students out to the suburbs. The suburban schools were not kind to those students – not a welcoming experience for a person of color. My parents wanted me to go there, Dad, especially. He wanted me to go to one of the best high schools the Twin Cities offered. Looking back at it through the eyes of a journalism and public policy major, he was probably rightfully against sending me to the same school he was trying to help fix. He wanted the best for all kids, but at the same time, the very best for his own kids." Amber's husband, Marcus Coleman, serves at a high level public federal staff position.

Joshua Moore, grandson

Joshua, Ramona's son, was born in 1975 and grew up in Minnesota. Bill had adopted his mother, so they're not related by blood. But Joshua is adamant – Bill is definitely his grandfather in all the most important ways.

"Grandpa's always been there for me, helping, advising, taking me to Minnesota Vikings games and introducing me to players like football legends Carl Eller and Alan Page," Joshua said. "It was always a lot of fun going over to his place on the weekends, just to hang out with Grandpa. Freddie was always good to me, too, and insisted we were all family. Besides, she's a phenomenal cook, which was a plus."

Joshua so excelled in high school that he spent his senior year attending junior college. He then enrolled at Clark Atlanta University in Atlanta, Georgia. He is currently the President and Chief Operating Officer of The Apparel Group, a U.S. distributor for one of the largest clothing manufacturers in the world.

"Nobody can touch my grandfather in terms of dressing snappy, but I try," Joshua quipped with a smile. "He was just 'Grandpa' when I was growing up. But he was often surrounded by these bigger-than-life Black men – businessmen, community leaders, etc. – who provided powerful role models for me. The Twin Cities Black community is relatively small, compared with other major metro areas. Finding role models can be tough for some kids. But I was lucky. Eventually, I learned that Grandpa had earned near legendary status locally and nationally. I always knew I wanted to be like him and the guys he hung out with."

Joshua, his wife LaKesha (Kesha) Moore and Bill

Even more memorable to Joshua than attending professional football games were the many times Bill showed up on the sidelines to watch him play sports. From the time Joshua was young, "Grandpa was one of those cool guys who would drive up in his shiny black Lexus. When I played football for Minneapolis Parks and Recreation, I could always find him in the bleachers because he dressed extremely nicely. I was very proud and knew I would have my best day on the field with him to cheer me on. He made the effort to come to events even my dad couldn't attend.

"He was not a typical grandfather," Joshua said. "He was the cool guy that everybody, young and old, wanted to be around. When I came home on college breaks, I was always going over to his and Freddie's place, especially on Sundays when we'd all watch football games together. I have three sons now and from the time my first baby was born, my wife and I continued the Sunday tradition.

"My first two years in college, I was all over the place in terms of what to study. By my sophomore year, I'd declared seven different majors. My grandfather said, 'Look, Josh. You need to figure out what you want to do.' I replied, 'That's the problem, Grandpa. I want to do too many things.' So he advised me in a way that made me feel like a certain direction was my idea. 'You're good with numbers. You have an affinity for business. How about finding a field that involves both?' So I double majored in finance and accounting, finished up in four years and graduated with a fantastic job waiting for me.

"I attribute a lot of what I'm doing today and my success to Grandpa's advice," Joshua said. "He was instrumental in my upbringing. He recognized the fact that I was a pretty headstrong young man, and respected my ideas. I could accept his advice because of the way he dispensed it – a gentle, yet firm influence. I attempt to emulate his approach with my three sons.

"I say this without reservation," Joshua concluded. "Grandpa is my hero."

Alec Moore (Joshua's middle son), Xavier Moore (Joshua's youngest son), Joshua, Grandpa Bill and Joshua, Jr., at Xavier's 2023 graduation.

Cliff and two of his children

Ramona's first son, Clifford, was also influenced by Bill during his formative years. After two years of college, he joined the Marine Corps and served proudly. He is a patriotic veteran, is currently an independent contractor and the father of three. He remains close to his grandfather.

PART 5

AFTERWARD
ACKNOWLEDGMENTS
&
ADDENDUM

AFTERWARD

"Like every race comprising the population of the United States, not all Black Americans have the same background," Bill said. "For instance, while some are American descendants of slavery, not all can trace their origins to the horrors of servitude. History indicates that there were independent Blacks in the U.S. as early as 1619. Other people, like Nigerians, Liberians, Somalis, Eritreans and Ethiopians who arrived since 1960, don't identify as African-Americans. Their nationality remains linked to their country of origin."

Bill's ancestors were slaves. The shackles are long since broken, but the strength it took to overcome bondage and the dignity of those who came before him courses uncompromisingly through his veins. He is never one to rest on laurels, but he does allow himself the occasional look back on the progress that's been made while he strategizes on making things better for generations to come.

Bill's legacy is not limited to his family. It also includes the countless people and programs he has lifted up and sustained.

"I sincerely hope that after reading my book, you will understand what informed my political points of view and propelled me into activism on behalf of justice, affordable healthcare and economic equalizers," Bill concluded.

ACKNOWLEDGMENTS

Bill refers to his first marriage as his "shotgun wedding" days. That's a description applied when premarital sex results in a pregnancy and the father of the bride supposedly stands by with a shotgun to ensure that nobody runs off and a wedding occurs. In Bill's, case, however, his mother was the one who applied the most pressure. "If you get a woman pregnant, you WILL marry her," Lorene told all of her sons early on. So when Bill's girlfriend became pregnant with his baby, he married her.

"During that time, I worked at an Elk's Club hotel/restaurant where I met a man named Paul Petersen," Bill said. "Paul spent 18 years in prison for a crime he didn't commit." Nearly two decades later, authorities found the real culprit and Paul was released. Fortunately, he had used his time of unjust incarceration learning to be a chef and preparing for a career on the outside.

"Paul called me 'Billy.' I didn't like that and told him so. He replied, 'Billy Boy, you ain't old enough to tell me what to call you. Now listen to me, Billy. You are very bright. You read a lot, speak well and could have a huge future. But first, you gotta take charge of your life and not be driven by knocking some girl up. So how many times are you gonna do that again? Get your act together. Finish your education and then look to the moon and shoot for the stars."

Bill took the older man's advice to heart and coupled it with what his mom told him, which was "Son, you owe."

Bill sites an old Nigerian proverb that states, "it takes the whole village to raise a child." He recently learned through DNA that he is 55-percent Nigerian and another 20-percent Benin, which is adjacent to Nigeria. "It has taken many various individuals and villages during each stage of my life, and continue to this very moment, that have shaped the man I am today," Bill said.

My many and distinct villages

Mahala Ward Griggs (Aunt Gay)
Maceo Ward (Uncle)
William Ward (Uncle) I was named to honor him.
Alice McCoy (Mom's Best Friend)
Laura "Nanny" Wellmaker
Julia Frances Green (Mom's other Best Friend)
Deacon Frank Hardy (Grandfather of Rev. Henry Hardy, one of my best friends and quoted in this book)
Mrs. Bessie Williams, Sunday school teacher who recognized I could read at age four

Middle years through high school and beyond (My "Best Friends")

Alfred Earl Lucas
George McCoy
Jessie Robinson
Robert "Flash" Hunter
Ruby Dale Hudson
Delores "Black Beauty" Johnson
Leona Jackson
Audrey Phillips
Loretta Glover
Shirley Green
Estelle Chatman
Althea Owens (her father ran a "juke joint")

Post high school\college\military years

Phyllis Roberts (1st wife)
Margurite Porter (bore a son for me)
Willie Davis
Leroy Hampton
Fred Lenoir
Richard "Cool Eyes" Brown
Paul Peterson
Percy Williams
Walter Wilkens
Bill Wade, Blue Devil's Band leader (I sang for them)
Cathy England
Jeannie Ware Adams (2nd wife)
Shirley Jean Hughes (3rd wife)
Freddie Lavern Davis-English (4th wife)

Those who influenced my civic and corporate lives

Dr. Josie Robinson Johnson
Charles "Chuck" Johnson
Stanley Rogers King
William "Bill" Bowman
George DeClouet
Bill Wilson
Paul Norman
Richard Green
Elder Mahmoud El Kati

My corporate village and supporters

Norbert Berg (my champion and protector for 32-plus years at Control Data)
Roger Wheeler (longtime direct supervisor – he taught Bill how to be an accomplished administrator)
Tom Linklater (Bill's first supervisor at CDC)
James "Jim" R. Morris (he was greatly influential in my growth)
Harley Feldman (nice boss, smart as a whip)
William "Bill" Fitzgerald (he saved my career and became a brother by another mother and whose beautiful wife **Emelia** and daughters **Leslie Fitzgerald Doll** [RIH] and **Carol Fitzgerald Tyler** [became family])

Those who hugely influenced my civic awakening and engagement

W. Harry Davis (a local giant and hugely influential in mine and other lives of Black Twin Citians)
Cecil Newman (publisher and editor of the Mpls. *Spokesman*, friend/advisor to Vice President Hubert Humphrey)
Earl Bowman
Edward Solomon
Chuck Cooper (first Black NBA player signed by the Boston Celtics)
Joyce Hughes (the first black woman to become a professor of law at the University of Minnesota, Fullbright Scholar, a member of the Helsinki Conservatory and a retired legendary professor of law at Northwestern University)
Dr. Retha Clark King
Robert Brunick (retired president of the University of Minnesota)
Robert J. Jones (Chancellor, University of Illinois)
Kathleen O'Brien
Sharon Sayles Belton (first female Black mayor of Minneapolis)
Larry Borom
Ernestine Belton
Steven Belton
Jeffery Hassan
Stella Whitney West
Dorothy Bridges
Lea Hargett
Tim and Doris Baylor (Tim is a major developer. His family owns more than 10 McDonald's franchises. He is a former Minnesota lieutenant governor candidate and demonstrates leadership and philanthropy through charitable giving. Doris is a leader in her own right and serves as a leader in the family businesses)
Ravi Norman (Ravi is one of the most brilliant minds Bill has ever known. He is a recognized regional business leader and is COO of his own company, Sagiliti)
Jill Stever-Zietlin
Tashitaa Tufaa (an extraordinary entrepreneur who happens to be a naturalized citizen from Ethiopia and a member of the Oromo Community. The proud owner of a transportation company that employees more than 300 employees in a multimillion-dollar business)
Keith Ellison (Minnesota State Attorney General)
Chanda Smith Baker (one in a million and my other surrogate niece by another adopted brother, her father, and a very close member of my extended family and village)
Louis King (CEO of OIC of America – his wife, **Beverly King,** is a long-time friend)

Special acknowledgments of my team who got the work done at Control Data and supported me

Herbert Pearl (Bill's best friend and adopted brother [RIH])
Cynthia Tyner (a loyal friend and great mother)
Geraldine Hollinsworth Jones
Fred Morgan
Sam Robinson
Phil Borom
Helen Lewis Wells
Jon "Rookie" Calloway
Debra Williams Jones
Suzanne Snyder

Special group of staff and teachers who supporter when I served as principal at the City Inc., an Alternative High School

Kate Benson, Pat Anderson, Stephen Ketter, Jon Sloan, Antonia Brown, Carla Bates Elizabeth Jappa

Special friends that continue to inform my life including my spiritual leaders

The Rev. Henry Orlando Hardy
Rev. Jerry McAfee
Rev, Randolph Staten
Rev. Ian Bethel
Bernadia Johnson
Dr. Timothy Childs

My closest village, my-siblings

Dan English Jr.
Thomas James English
Helen Ma'Dean English
Alfred Clark English
Althea English Williams

Marian English Cunningham
Maurice "Pete: English
Edward English
Josheph English
Charles English (my ride and die brother)
Rita English
Martha English

My children

William "Butch" English, Jr.
Ramona English
Cheryl Denise English
Charles "Bubby" Porter
Amber Nicole English Coleman

My grandchildren and great grandchildren

William English III
Tasha English
Clifford Moore
Joshua Moore
Tanika English
Jabraun Miller
Joshua Moore II
Alexia Moore
Brooklyn Moore
Drake Moore
Alec Moore
Xavier Moore
Azalia Anderson

★ A special thanks to Ralph Hargrow, long-time friend and great C-suite corporate executive. Ralph gave Bill the name of this book and he is forever grateful.

ADDENDUM

I sincerely hope the readers of this book understand that it is not an autobiography. Black culture dictates that we don't tell all. Some things are private. In circumspect, I have been in therapy for several years and it has brought me understanding of my behaviors, both good and bad. I urge any Black male readers of this book to seek therapy. And I hope it's as helpful to you as it has been for me.

The following are awards that I was honored to receive and mean a great deal to me.

- *Minnesota Women's Political Caucus Fair Players Honoree 1989*

- *Who's Who Amoung Black Americans 1977 - 1978 2nd Edition*

- *Coalition of Black Churchies Lifetime Achievement Award 2000*

- *African American Leadership Forum Community Service Award 2018*

ADDITIONAL THOUGHTS

This book was not my idea. Rather, it was the brainchild of Norbert R. Berg, retired Control Data Corporation (CDC) Executive Vice President and Deputy Chairman of the Board. This generous man decided that my story, which in my mind is not remarkable, should be told.

After serious prayer and discussions with my family and a few long-time friends and colleagues, I decided with much reluctance to tell my story in the hope that it would inspire any young man, particularly American Descendants of Slavery, that their circumstance is not their destiny.

Freddie

My life. My love. My reason.

Norb Berg

Most CDC employees knew that Norb was closer to and more respected by Bill Norris, founder and CEO, than any of the other C-suite executives. Norb is a great humanitarian and was the genius behind most of CDC's innovative Human Resource programs. From my and others' observations, Bill Norris clearly trusted Norb on other Control Data matters, including acquisitions, divestitures and the financial issues facing any competitors in the supercomputer field. He helped take the company from nearly scratch to a $4-billion enterprise with 65.000 employees worldwide. Norb hired me, supported me and together with Roger Wheeler, allowed me to make an impact on CDC's diversity advances and serve my community without fear of repercussions from my employer. My family and I are very grateful to Norb for his generosity, faith in me for more than 32 years, and continuing friendship and camaraderie.

Cavitt Productions

To the Cavitt sisters who wrote this book. I am so appreciative of their willingness to hear me and capture on paper the authenticity of my story. They displayed so much patience in my missing deadlines. At times, I was more than a little embarrassed by my delays, but they simply reassured me, offered encouragement and drove the project ahead. Thank you, Tina and Geni. You are two amazing writers with the patience of Job. I am proud of your work and you two are always in my favor.

A FEW MORE ACKNOWLEDGMENTS

After reading and approving the final draft, I realized I left out people who helped me on my journey. It would be a serious error of omission if I did not mention these important individuals in my village.

First, my other sibling (how I forgot one brother is beyond me): **Lafayette "Pepper" English**.

On page 128, I mention **Chanda Smith Baker**. I want to acknowledge her a little differently. I should have stated the following: As a member of my extended family (informally adopted), she has had considerable influence on my thinking. She is intellectually brilliant and intuitively connected to her community. Chanda is a true thought leader – down-to-earth and very straightforward. There is no b.s. in her being. She is one in a million.

Always,
–Bill

ABOUT CAVITT PRODUCTIONS

As they grew up, the Cavitt sisters learned to value stories woven by their older relatives. Eventually, Geni moved west to work in San Diego radio and television. Christina stayed in the Midwest to write business communications and biographies. They discovered how well their gifts blended when they teamed up to create a photo-video legacy project in 2009, so they kept at it, eventually writing books.

The Cavitts are grateful to Bill who opened his door to them, generously sharing his wisdom, humor and wonderful stories. They are also grateful to Norb Berg, who inspired this project. And they thank their creative director, Francha Cavitt.

www.ingramcontent.com/pod-product-compliance
Lightning Source LLC
Chambersburg PA
CBHW051319120626
46547CB00015B/2312